THE
MESSENGER WITHIN

*Discovering Love and Wholeness
Through Meditation*

SORAYA SUSAN BEHBEHANI

Mellen Research University Press
San Francisco

Library of Congress Cataloging-in-Publication Data

Behbehani, Soraya Susan.
    The messenger within : discovering love and wholeness through
meditation / Soraya Susan Behbehani.
       p.   cm.
    Includes bibliographical references.
    ISBN 0-7734-9882-6
    1. Sufism. 2. Maktab Tarighat Oveyssi Shahmaghsoudi. I. Title.
BP189.6.B44   1991
297'.43--dc20
                                       91-28177
                                          CIP

For editorial inquiries contact:

Mellen Research University Press
534 Pacific Avenue
San Francisco
CA 94133

To place orders, contact:

The Edwin Mellen Press
P.O. Box 450
Lewiston
NY 14092

Printed in the United States of America

Knowledge is the priceless heritage of mankind

TABLE OF CONTENTS

ACKNOWLEDGEMENT

Fifteen years ago destiny led me to the school of Islamic Sufism, where I met the most knowledgeable, lovable and the kindest man I had ever known. He was **Hazrat Shah Maghsoud Sadegh Angha**, the spiritual teacher of the Oveyssi School of Sufism, in Sufi-Abad, Karaj, Iran. There, for the first time I became acquainted with Sufism, the reality of religion.

Like a child I was completely mystified at the presence of **Hazrat Shah Maghsoud Sadegh Angha,** and felt a tranquility and warmth I had never felt before. I dedicated more and more time in an effort to repeat that rare new experience, which I could neither understand nor explain but which I had found so nourishing. Later I knew that it was my soul he had touched.

When he was no more in his physical being on earth I thought the light was extinguished for ever. It was not until I began my practical training under his son, the current leader and teacher of The Oveyssi School of Sufism **Hazrat Salaheddin Ali Nader Angha**, that I learned that the light was the light of God that never dies but is always present in different manifestations to guide and enlighten the yearning soul. I also found that the path to truth is an inner path and its guide is the messenger within.

I am very proud to have been trained personally by the great Sufi master of our time **Hazrat Salaheddin Ali Nader Angha.** It has been under his loving care and instruction that my growth and the development of my inner potentials have taken place. Through him I have received the gift of spiritual love and life; I am very grateful to him for showing me a better and more fulfilling way of life.

His teachings are mammoth and in this book I have only been able to skim the surface. The ocean of truth is so vast and deep that I am still learning and hope that this book will encourage the readers to do the same.

I would like to thank my sister Mandana Behbehani, for her help toward the publication of this book and my dear friend Tom Elmore for his beautiful introduction. Again, I would like to thank **Hazrat Salaheddin Ali Nader Angha** for always being there, caring, guiding and teaching, to whom I owe everything.

Soraya Behbehani
September, 30

AUTHOR'S PROFILE

Soraya is a stress management specialist, who has been teaching Sufi meditation and stress management techniques nationally and internationally since 1981. She has held numerous workshops and seminars at community colleges and universities and for the general public at large. She is also a healer, who has conducted magnetic therapy with class participants with wide range of psychological and somatic illnesses such as cancer.

Soraya is involved in extensive research into the physical and behavioral effects of meditation the data of which is collected from her ongoing classes with large number of participants.

Born in Lansing, Michigan, Soraya was raised in Iran and England. She was educated in Europe and in the U.S., and speaks several languages including French, English, German, Spanish, and Persian. She has received her bachelor degree in philosophy and religion, and is professionally certified in health promotion management and consulting through the University of California at San Diego. Soraya is currently working on her Doctoral degree in clinical psychology, specializing in holistic health psychology.

The most important part of her training and what makes her quite unique in her field is her spiritual training by the eminent Sufi Master of our time, Hazrat Salaheddin Ali Nader Shah Angha, Pir, Oveyssi. Not only has His Holiness directed and guided her through her theoretical and practical training in the science of Sufism and Self knowledge but has been the force behind all her achievements.

She now lives in San Diego and is currently the chairperson of the department of meditation and healing of MTO Shah Maghsoudi, the Oveyssi School of Islamic Sufism.

"I remember so vividly the rare and wondrous luncheon I had with you at the AACD Convention in Los Angeles in 1986. It was a moment of magic to be in your presence. You have an air of serenity, and genuine peace, an inner depth and beauty, which shines like a star in the mist. It was wonderful to share with you concerning matters of the spirit and heart, and to learn from you about Sufism."

– Tom Elmore
Director of Counselor Education and Professor of Counseling
Psychology. Wake Forest University, Noth Carolina

"Stress has been shown to weaken the body's inmune system. As a participant, I find the MTO meditation classes highly effective in combating physical and mental stress and I highly recommend people to take these classes for better health and as a measure of preventive medicine."

– Dr. Ravin Agah M.D.
Specialist in contagious and terminal diseases at University of
Southern California Medical Center, July 11, 1988

INTRODUCTION

A bird of paradise has written a love song to the world and signed it SORAYA. Not only has Soraya written the words of the song, she teaches us how to sing them through meditation in order to produce a universal harmony.

Properly rendered, the biblical scriptures say that "In the beginning God, the divine energy of Love, was in the process of expressing herself." It is a process without beginning or end, manifested in time, but embedded in eternity. This is the message of Sufism, a process which so predates human history that its beginning is lost in time, but is the basis of all truth. It is something more than mere religious belief, theology, philosophy, or psychology, although these human inventions may point toward its reality.

In this book Soraya explains the basis and true nature of Sufism and the reality of the Messenger within. But more than that she moves beyond ideology to the methodology of meditation. However, she explains that meditation is not so much a method, technique, learned skill, or what one does as it is what a person lets happen. It is a surrender, an emptying, a transcending of the demands and desires of the transient or temporal self, an opening to Being itself. As such, it is all that there is to know, because Being or God is in itself the One and All.

In relation to the profession of counseling with which the present author is most familiar, meditative surrender in the Sufi sense is not consistent with forms of behaviorism which seek to shape behavior. Neither can such meditation be equated to psychoanalytic free association by which in-the-moment is often missing. Soraya helps us to move beyond theoretical knowledge about the rose of religion to smelling its scent. Again, for her, religion must be experience marked by innocence of perception. You must become like children to enter the Kingdom of God.

While Soraya describes methods for gaining physical balance and bodily alignment, her intention is to achieve the purpose of soul alignment. The power of the Messenger within is always there to be accessed. That is our job. Largely, we create our bodily and mental problems and we have the capacity to create paths to where the solution rests, within. Soraya outlines a method for becoming aware of stressors which block our path to wholeness and cites relaxation methods for reaching moments between thoughts in order to achieve peace.

Most importantly, Soraya believes that one must go beyond body and mind and address concerns of the Spirit which asks existential questions about the meaning of life, such as; Who am I? Why am I? and What is the purpose of life?

The "holy cloak" of Islamic Sufism is explained by Soraya in tracing the history of the cloak-bearers from the prophet Abraham to Hazrat Mohammed, and from him to Hazrat Salaheddin Ali Nader Angha, the spiritual guide of the School of Islamic Sufism. However, she explains that the heart of each individual person can hear the "Angelic Voice" of God and find his or her Messenger and Savior within the innermost part of the soul where God, the only true guide, dwells.

This is the claim of Islamic Sufism, that each person must grasp intuitively through mystical experience the truth of existence for himself or herself. Our real identity is the "I" beyond the temporal ego or personality. Our essence is timeless. The highest wisdom is mystery, something to be experienced, not rationally known in an earthly sense. Thus, ultimately, Sufism in its deeper meaning cannot be defined.

In brief, the Sufi seeks unity with the Divine which is achieved through the ecstacy of Love and self-abandonment. The stages of religious development proceed from obtaining the Law, walking the Way, and through total surrender finding the Truth. This involves a remembrance of God, a remembrance which impels a journey by the seeker from the outer world to the world within.

In Carl Jung's psychology and Joseph Campbell's mythology, this is the mythic hero/heroine journey, the universal cosmic round everywhere present in all persons and cultures. Sufi meditation is then a means to discover the Truth hidden in experience and to achieve communion with God. This meditation requires an inner transformation which is wrought by the most elevated experience of love.

Soraya invites us to experience the ecstasy of love and to surrender to the source of life. To follow our metaphor, she calls on all to spread their wings and start their journey and flight back home, a home that is no further away than within.

Tom Elmore
Director of Counselor Education and
Professor of Counseling Psychology
Wake Forest University

PART ONE

PART ONE

INTRODUCTION

With many schools of meditation offering diverse approaches today, people may become confused about which one they should choose in the field of self-development. The question I am asked most frequently is "Out of the many classes I could attend, how do I know which one to choose?"

It is only natural that one should have knowledge about something before making any choices. There are so many misconceptions both about what one can achieve through meditation and about meditation itself that a new student should gather information and examine it closely before beginning.

For example, since drug experiences and meditation are described as consciousness-expanding, one can mistakenly assume that consciousness expands the same way in both these cases and thus produces the same effect. This was true in the case of a young student of mine who turned to meditation as a release from an alcohol and drug addiction. He expected the same results he had experienced with drugs, envisioning vivid colors and fantasies or feeling "high."

Others, who are more oriented toward problem-solving, think of meditation as contemplation. They believe meditation consists of sitting quietly and focusing the mind on a particular problem in order to resolve or at least gain deeper insight into it. There is nothing wrong with this, but it is not what meditation is. In the West, the terms *meditation* and *contemplation* are often interchanged, but in the East, the practice of meditation is distinct from that of contemplation.

By others, whose thinking is more careless and scattered, meditation may be imagined as simply a process of letting the mind drift from one thought to another. However, as with an undirected boat on the ocean, this erratic drifting will lead nowhere. Sooner or later, winds and tides will haphazardly move the boat, but more often than not, they will not take us where we want or need to go. Many people live their lives in this uncertain way.

If one truly and correctly experiences, one will understand right away that it is an experience very different from those described above. The purpose of meditation is not to get high or to have unusual experiences. Although some students report seeing colors and visions, a competent teacher will usually discourage them from becoming too interested in these distracting forms and colors. The expansion of consciousness should result in *an increase of energy, alertness, and an improvement of abilities*, not the altered perceptions caused by drugs, which cause a chemical imbalance in the brain.

Chemical imbalance can cause mistaken depth perception. For example, because eyes cannot see depth, the brain calculates one's distance from an object with the help of available clues through the eyes and also experiences. However, a person under the influence of certain drugs will not be able to perceive that distance. Drug abuse, therefore, is clearly not an expansion of consciousness nor even of sensual perception. Mistaking the effects of meditation for those of drug abuse means not knowing *what meditation really is*.

Nor is meditation a form of thinking, of letting one's mind float or daydreaming. Meditation goes beyond sensory experiences, beyond haphazard movement, along a path which enriches life and gives it purpose and direction. Meditation has a definite goal.

The Messenger Within, unlike information found in most available books on this subject, has a wide perspective. This book is not addressed to the narrow interests of a particular group but is a complete survey of the origins, theories, and practice of meditation. To make it more comfortable for the reader, I have divided the information in this book into three parts.

In Part One, I will discuss the history of meditation and its practice according to different traditions and religions. Part Two will consider stress and stress-management. In Part Three, each religion will be brought together under the reality of religion, Sufism, which unites them all.

When the last stage of religion, *Islam*, meaning *surrender* is reached, *Adam*, the child of light, is born into the infinite. Breaking away from sensory boundaries in a complete surrender, he leaves behind his limited existence and finally unites with his purpose in life through the act of true meditation.

In reality this is a spiritual journey that takes place in the soul, a journey that takes man from a limited being to a boundless and unlimited being. The essence of existence is an infinite knowledge, abstractly called *God*. It is this very essence that molds and gives birth to all things. However, this essence that is man's true self has temporarily become trapped in the solid human form. Like a pearl that remains hidden inside its shell, man's true identity has become bound by the limitations of the earth. In order to stop the yearning and alienation of the suffering soul, the infinite essence or the speck of light must break away from the limitations of the body into the existence and unite with infinity. As a drop of water is but water in a limited form, once it reaches the ocean, it is no longer a solitary drop but part of the ocean.

The Sufi practice, meditation and remembrance of God *(Zekr)* will lead the Sufi to his beloved, *his true identity*. This "realization" can only be attained through the understanding and practice of the *one message* of religion. Each and every one of the Messengers of God – Zoroaster, Buddha, Moses, Jesus, and Mohammad – represents a different stage of this one Message: "know thyself." The different stages of understanding are Zoroastrianism, Buddhism, Judaism, Christianity, and in its final stage, Islam.

To "know thyself" is to find that which you have been searching for all your life... yourself. This is a healing process that takes place once we have come in touch and harmony with our true and single being. Once we have discovered such purpose in our lives, we can grow. Ralph Waldo Emerson

CHAPTER ONE

SCIENCE AND MEDITATION

Words do not convey meaning.

Hazrat Shah Maghsoud Sadegh Angha

Why have most of us forgotten the "whys" we asked as children? Where does the wind blow from? Where does the elegance, order, and grace of a new blossom come from? In which part of that harsh wooden branch or dark interlaced roots was this colorful, delicate, elegant and fragrant flower hidden? And two questions we never ask anymore: Where is God? What is the purpose of creation?

People who readily accept all things remain ignorant. The most obstinate and questioning minds are always the most intuitive, for they have not lost their sense of wonder. People who keep questioning do not take anything for granted; their minds have not become hard and static. Let us broaden our perspective and open our minds: Let us look at meditation with the eyes of a child.

Let us be scientific in our approach. A scientist analyzes by observation and experimentation. Ideally, science aims and searches for the truth, and puts nothing on the scales until it can offer objective evidence and verification.

Opinions, on the other hand, offer themselves to be accepted or rejected and promise no evidence, truth, or certainty. Opinions and personal impressions are therefore not reliable. Even the most reasonable opinion may only be the first step toward an established reality. Therefore, scientists do not presume, assume, fantasize, or philosophize; their claims are well-supported and backed by tests, experimentation, and practical evidence gained in the laboratory.

In our investigations, let us combine the open minds of children and the searching minds of the scientist. Clearly, the results of scientific investigations are firm and reliable because they are based on observation and practice. Anything but the practical method described above is not scientifically accepted. Similarly, religion has to be understood by investigation and practical evidence,...not blind faith. To the unsupported, unscientific mind, the world of religion can seem to be a realm of pure opinion and even of fabrication. Religion claims that "seeing is believing". As Hafiz, the well-known Sufi poet who despised pharisaism once said,

> Since the Truth was not realized,
> It seemed best to fantasize.

Religion should be the pursuit of Truth that leads to direct experience of what the Truth actually is, not one that results in personal opinions and fabrications. Such fabrications are self-made and imaginary and can be subject to continual change, as one changes. A God that I create within my mind is not real, but my own creation. In the language of science this is called a *hypothesis*. It is not a proven fact backed by evidence. Such religion is merely based on everything I have heard from others plus my own imagination and inventions. Whereas religion should be known on the basis of individual experience of Truth and reality. One might even wonder if there really is that much difference between the one who accepts religion upon blind faith, and another that rejects it. Lack of true knowledge is the result in both cases, since one has rejected it without knowing, the other has accepted without knowing and blindly, as "blind faith" applies.

Religion has come to be equated with belief systems, dogma, rituals, forms of practice, and organizational structure. Too often spiritual truths announced by the prophets have been obscured and distorted with emphasis on claims of scriptural inerrancy, and literal rather than spiritual interpretation of their teachings. "Religio" comes from a verb meaning "to bind together." Religion, thus, is that inner imperative which compels a person to bind together everything in a harmonious whole. But how differently the word has now been misused in practice.

The history of religion is therefore a very sad one. The prophet Mohammad and his teachings were very different from what is known as the religion of Islam today. Jesus Christ's beliefs, too, were different from Christianity as we know it today. If Jesus Christ were to show up today at the gates of the Vatican, he would be very surprised to see what was going on. Today, religious institutions are not representatives of the real teachings of the prophets.

All religion today is little more than tradition. It has become a combination of different religious and folk ceremonies portraying not the Truth but a collection of myths, tales, and symbols. It is a replay and imitation of past historical events without the reasons as to *why* they were performed in the first place and *what* is gained by their repetition. Religion practiced in this manner cannot lead to true faith and belief, but rather *make-believe*. Religion has very seldom been truly and scientifically investigated.

Although physical tools cannot measure metaphysics, there has to be a manner of investigation that will lead us to faith, certainty, and confidence. The Sufis point out that careful exploration and experimentation lead to the Truth, and that we must learn to go beyond *words* to find the reality behind the now-empty ceremonies and symbols of religion. For "Words do not convey meaning,"[1] but are only signs that represent ideas. Our understanding of the word is based on experience; without that experience, words are just words, not meaning.

Mere words, like religious ideas, are of little use; we are constantly using words without actually understanding or closely examining them. "Water" is communicated only among those who know what water is. Simple names have become too familiar to arouse our curiosity and lead us to investigate and comprehend the complexities that lie beneath them. What is "love," for example, and how can we truly define it? Where does it come from, amid all this chemical action and reaction of the body? Where is its source? The same is true of the words "God" and "Truth." We fight and kill over religious ideas and opinions, yet they are so unclear, so unknown, so meaningless, and so changeable. The evolution of the soul, the purpose of religion, cannot be attained by the repetition of such abstract symbols as words.

Jesus Christ said:

'Knock and the door will be opened.'
(Matthew 7:7)

Have we ever asked which door it is that he speaks of? How are we to find that door, that gateway? And how are we supposed to knock?

Through meditation, self-exploration takes place. All the prophets preach about this self-exploration. The message is an old one and does not belong to any particular tradition, sect, or religion but includes and unites them all. The more the message is understood, the more we will realize the similarities between the various faiths. Even books on meditation make a distinction between the meditation practiced in the West and that practiced and understood in the East. But the distinctions we see are products of different cultures, traditions, and philosophies developed in separate regions with relation to geographical and historical factors. It is as if we are all looking at the same landscape through different windows; these sociocultural windows, like stained glass, are full of designs representing our thoughts and prejudices, but which color and distort our view.

Zoroaster, Buddha, Moses, Jesus and Mohammad, the wise prophets, all repeat the same message. It is the transformation of that *one message* that is worth considering.

Thousands of instruments, a different tune each plays.
When heard from deep within,
The same sweet melody each portrays.[2]

Or as the Persian poet Ganjavi says:

The Truth you may recognize not,
Among the many ornaments lost.[3]

Let us start our investigation into meditation by looking at dictionary definitions of meditation.

Dictionary Definitions of Meditation:

Roots: Latin-meditat, stem of meditari, from the root med., meaning "thought" or "care."

"Meditation" is defined:

- by *Webster's New World Dictionary* as:
  1) Act of meditating; deep continued thought.
  2) Deep reflection on sacred matters as a devotional act.

- by *Nattall's Standard Dictionary* as:
  Continued attention to a particular subject.

- by *Funk and Wagnalls Standard Desk Dictionary* as:
  The act of meditating; reflection upon a subject; contemplating.

"Meditate" is defined as:

- by *The Oxford Advanced Learner's Dictionary of English* as:
  Think about; consider; give oneself up to serious

  thought.

- by *The Oxford Universal Dictionary on Historical Principles* as:
  To reflect upon; to study; ponder; to observe with intentness; to plan by revolving in the mind; to design mentally;
  to think; to exercise the mind (esp. devotional) thought or contemplation, and

  "Meditation" as:

  Serious reflection or mental contemplation.

  Special in religious use: The continuous application of the mind to the contemplation of some religious truth, mystery, or object of reverence, as a devotional exercise.

These definitions apply to "concentration" and "contemplation" rather than "meditation." It is not by the help of the mind that the "mystery of humanity" unravels itself. Meditation goes beyond the mind. However, "concentration" is the preliminary step towards "meditation."

Different schools of meditation have been subject to the misunderstanding of the original one message brought to man: "Know thyself." These differences may confuse the beginning student: *Is meditation one practice or many?* There seems to be many different forms of meditation. He hears about Zen meditation, Transcendental meditation, Yoga meditation, and other varieties. He learns that while the *Zen Buddhist monk* sits quietly with his eyes partially opened, looking at a blank wall, the *yoga meditator* sits with his eyes closed, concentrating on a particular *word, thought, or image.* To understand the apparent differences among forms of meditation, we must study carefully the historical roots of the religions from which these forms blossomed.

CHAPTER ONE ENDNOTES

1.   Molana Shah Maghsoud Sadegh Angha; refer to the introduction of *Manifestation of Thought*.

2.   Hafiz, Persian Sufi poet.

3.   Ganjavi Nizami, Persian Sufi poet.

CHAPTER TWO

THE ANCIENT RELIGIONS OF IRAN AND INDIA: ZOROASTRIANISM AND HINDUISM

*Rightful Deed, Rightful Thought,
and Rightful Speech.*

Basic Teachings, Zoroaster

Where does our story begin? One might as well ask where truth begins. Our historical background is as old as humanity.

We will begin with the prophet who is famous for spending long years meditating in the forest, the *Buddha*. Buddha lived at a time when the major *Upanishads*,[1] a series of mystical texts pertaining to the Hindu philosophy, were already in existence. Their philosophy must be seen as the point of departure for his own teaching. It would be a serious mistake, however, to look upon Buddha as the "founder" or "reformer" of a religion that came into being as some kind of organized revolt against Hinduism, for we are speaking of a time when there was no consciousness of "religions," when such terms as "Hinduism" or "Brahmanism" would have meant nothing. There was simply a tradition, embodied in the orally transmitted doctrine of the Veda and Upanishads, a tradition that was not specifically "religious"; it involved a whole way of life and concerned everything from the methods of agriculture to the knowledge of the *ultimate reality*. To understand the philosophy of Buddha, we have to trace history back to 2500 B.C.

From the middle of the third millennium B.C. to the second millennium B.C. there was a thriving city civilization in Northwest India called the Indus Valley civilization. It came to an abrupt end around 1500 B.C., at about the time waves of *Aryans*, a nomadic warlike people, migrated into the area from western Asia and parts of the Mediterranean region. In Sanskrit, the word *Arya*[2] means nobles. Their language is also called *Aryan* and is the basis of all Indo and European languages. Hinduism has traditionally looked to the *Aryans* and their religion as its source and inspiration. Though many aspects of later Hinduism may well have been inspired by the Indus Valley civilization or regional peasant cultures in India, the earliest scriptures of the Aryans, the *Veda*, have been acknowledged for thousands of years as the embodiment of the primordial truths upon which Hinduism is based.

About 1000 B.C., Aryans moved into Iran from the north and northwest and by 800 B.C. they had occupied the land. These invaders brought a rich oral tradition, much of which is preserved in the Hindu *Rig-Veda* and the *Avesta* of Zoroastrianism. Thus the religions of India and Iran, both under Aryan influence, display a number of similar characteristics.

"Iran, or Persia, as it was once called," according to *The World Religions*,

> is enclosed within a triangle of mountains and has at its heart two salt deserts that are so barren that the Gobi Desert appears fertile in comparison. With the mountains towering to a height of 5,500 meters (18,000 feet), Iran is a land of great contrasts: tropical jungle near the Caspian Sea and Mediterranean climate in the river valleys of the Southwest. These differences have given rise to various cultures, and the mountains have impeded communication between the different cultures. While Western Iran is subject to influence from Mesopotamia, Greece, and Rome, the East is under the influence of India and even China. Iran thus stands as a bridge between East and West, not only influencing her religion, but making Iran a watershed of history as well.[3]

Having started out on common ground with India under the influence of the Aryans, the religion of Iran later became independent and established as *Zoroastrianism*. This religion was founded by *Zoroaster* (Zarathushtra in ancient Persian and Zardusht in modern Persian), the ancient Persian religious reformer. There is much controversy about the period in which he

lived. According to *World Religions: From Ancient History to the Present,*
Zoroaster lived from 628-551 B.C. or earlier. *Dictionary of Religions* says,
"Recent Parsi tradition dates him around 6,000 BCE [before Christian era]
but this date is not accepted by any Western academic. Instead, a date
around the 6th century BCE has been preferred although recent research
suggests an earlier date of 1700-1400 BCE as more likely."[4] The
Encyclopedia Britannica[5] notes that even the ancient Greeks named dates
thousands of years apart. "The Avesta,"[6] the scriptures of Zoroastrianism, "is
indeed our principal source for the doctrine of Zoroaster; on the subject of
his person and his life it is comparatively reticent; with regard to his date of
birth, it is absolutely silent. The 13th section, or *Spend Nask,* which was
mainly consecrated to the description of his life, has perished."

The uncertainty of the dates makes it difficult to know if Zoroaster's
doctrines came before the *Veda* or after. *Veda* means "sacred knowledge."
The *Veda* are documents held to be divine revelation; their oldest parts date
from about the middle of the second millennium B.C. They form the core of
Brahmanism, the system of religious doctrines and institutions of the
Brahman caste in Hinduism.

Originating with the *Veda,* the *Brahman* tradition developed into a
pantheistic concept involving the search for a unifying principle or single
spiritual reality called Brahman. The *Veda* maintain that our thoughts,
feelings, ideas, mental states, and even the soul are continuously changing;
this constant movement proves that life has no absolute stability or
permanence. However, deep within existence, like the seed or core within a
fruit as it blossoms, ripens, withers, and dies, lies a timeless Being called *sat,*
which never changes. "We have the direct experience, however vague, of this
being in the uttermost depths of our existence: *"We feel that we are."*[7] "For I
am one and the same person yesterday, today, and the day after, the same
person from childhood to death, in spite of the changes."[8] The individual's
experience of the ultimate self and ground of his existence is called *Atman.*

Atman is a Sanskrit word, the earlier meaning of which according to
the *Veda* is 'breath,' but whose later meaning is 'soul' or 'the absolute.' This
ultimate self, or Atman, in the individual is an ever-abiding, timeless being
that is "smaller than the small and greater than the great,"[9] and is stable.

The Ultimate Being is not an unconscious, unintelligent Being, but is *awareness* (chit) itself. The essential nature of being is *Love* (ananda), a love which is the root of all joy, peace, and bliss. Who indeed would move, would breathe, if there were not this *ananda* buried deep within every heart? For He alone makes life joyous and happy, and blissful and loving.

The Atman, the Ultimate Self in man, is pure *Being* (sat), objectless *awareness* (chit) and *Love* (ananda). Timeless and spaceless the Ultimate Being is only one being–one Atman in all individuals. This experience of the one Being has been reported by many true seers in other parts of the world, who have been vaguely called *Mystics* or *Sufis*.[10]

According to the *Veda*, the whole universe is one, and the one Atman is always present and gives birth to all things. "This the Atman does in a manner somewhat like that of a single vital cell multiplying itself into countless numbers."[11] The Atman marches away from his true state until his appearance as the physical is reached and becomes trapped in man's physical mold. Atman then becomes forgetful of himself and becomes the limited "I," the individual ego. The ego, the limited "I," therefore, begins again to seek out this lost vision. The vision can, however, no longer appear as a whole, but has buried within himself not only Atman, but also the previous states. The universe produced from the one undivided Atman is thus a unified system, a mighty organism in which the inmost nucleus and pervading Spirit and Self is the one abiding Being. The Atman lies within each particle of the universe; there can be no division in the Being, no real limitation to him in space, time, or any other way.

This is why the Hindu maintains that the *Vedic* seers were telling nothing but the simple truth when they declare that they perceived life and awareness in and behind every part and phenomenon of nature, visible and invisible. The seers called each manifestation a *Deva*. The *Devas*, crudely and incorrectly interpreted as *"Gods,"* but more properly *"angels,"* are thus not mere personifications of nature and its phenomena, but the very Spirit and Self of the Universe seen through Nature's forms as through a prism.[12]

While the doctrines of Brahmanism are *monistic* (based on the concept of *oneness*) those of Zoroaster propose *"duality."*[13] Zoroaster, one of the finest teachers of the East, greatly influenced the early Greek philosophers and writers.[14] He is said to have withdrawn himself from people to live alone upon a mountain. After a long period of contemplative solitude, he received an inward call addressed to him by God, who chose him to seek the amelioration of mankind and their deliverance from ruin.

Zoroaster's teachings have come down to us in seventeen hymns, *The Gathas*.[15] According to the *Encyclopedia Britannica*, his doctrine was rooted in the old Iranian, or Aryan, folk religion. Zoroaster, with all his inherent Iranian national character, shows his strong faith, boldness, and energy through his teachings. His thinking is consecutive, self-restrained and practical. His form of expression is tangible and concrete; his system is constructed on a clearly conceived plan and stands on a high moral level, and must have been a great advance in human civilization.

Zoroastrianism has a strong social ethic and, in contrast to Hinduism, an essentially activist one. However, although work is viewed as the *salt of life*, a person expresses his character not only with what he does and says but also with his thoughts. People must "overcome doubts and unrighteous desires with reason, overcome greed with contentment, anger with serenity, envy with benevolence, want with vigilance, strife with peace, falsehood with truth."[16] His basic teaching is:

"Rightful deed, rightful thought, and rightful speech."

According to Zoroaster, when the world began there existed two spirits who represented *the Good* and *the Evil*.[17] Both spirits possessed creative power that manifested itself positively in one and negatively in the other. *Ahura Mazda* is light and life, and creates all that is pure and good in the ethical world of law, order, and truth. His antithesis, *Ahriman* (devil), is darkness, filth, death, and produces all that is evil in the world. The two spirits counterbalance each other. The ultimate triumph of the good spirit is an ethical demand of Zoroaster's religion. Thus, Zoroaster's religion is the story of God's conflict with the Devil. The battlefield is man's soul. By a true confession of faith, by every good thought, word, and deed, by continually keeping his body and soul pure, man reduces the power of Satan and strengthens the might of goodness; he thus has the power to defeat *Ahriman* and to establish a claim for reward upon *Ahura Mazda*. Conversely by every evil deed, word, and thought, man allows his body and soul to be corrupted and defiled increasing evil and rendering service to Satan.

The Zoroastrians worshiped fire as a symbol and son of *Ahura Mazda*. Neither the sun nor unbelieving eyes must see the fire, and it is preserved in a fire-temple. When the Parsis (Persians) visit the fire, they kneel and bow as a sign of respect and their foreheads are marked with the ash as a symbol of humility and equality.

The influence of Zoroaster has been felt since ancient times and is still evident in modern religion and philosophy.

> Despite the small number of practicing Zoroastrians in the world today (just over 125,000 in India and, according to a 1976 census, 25,000 in Iran), Iranian religion, especially Zoroastrianism, has in fact played one of the major roles on the stage of world religious history. Zoroaster was much respected in Greece at the time of Plato, and the worship of *Mithras*[18] spread throughout the Roman Empire as far as northern England. Turning to the East, Iranian art and religion has long been a source of influence for India. Worship of Mithras spread from Iran to the Magas of India in the 6th century and later, but before that, Zoroastrianism may well have stimulated the growth of a savior concept in Buddhism, in the form of Maitreya Buddha. Iran has played a particularly important role in the religion of Islam, helping it develop from an Arab religion into an international religion. The growth of the mystical movement, the Sufis, and the savior concept may owe a lot to Iranian influence. Perhaps Iran's greatest influence has been on the development of Judeo-Christian belief. It is widely accepted by biblical scholars that the later Jewish concepts of the devil, hell, the afterlife, the resurrection, the end of the world, and the savior imagery – the very foundation of Christianity – were all colored by Zoroastrian beliefs. Theologically as well as geographically, Iran, the bridge between the East and West, has contributed immensely to the world's religions.[19]

CHAPTER TWO ENDNOTES

1.   *Upanishads,* "to sit near (the master)," a series of 108 mystical texts that are the basis of the six systems of Hindu philosophy. The *Upanishads* form the concluding portion of the *Veda*, the sacred texts of Hinduism. The early sections of the *Upanishads* were composed in the 8th century B.C. but the later parts are of a more recent date. The *Encyclopedia International,* p. 158.

2.   The Nazi dictator Adolf Hitler, who ruled Germany, used the word "Aryans" to mean Germans and certain other peoples of Northern Europe. He claimed that the Germans were the purest Aryans and therefore superior to all other peoples. Hitler used his ideas about Aryan supremacy to justify the killing of millions of Jews, Gypsies and other "non-Aryans."

3.   Parrinder, Geoffrey, *World Religions: From Ancient History to the Present,* Facts on File Publications, New York, New York, 1971, p. 177.

4.   John R. Hinnells, *Dictionary of Religions,* p. 361.

5.   Hermodorus and Hermippus of Smyrna place him 5,000 years before the Trojan War; Xanthus, 6,000 years before Xeres, Eudoxus and Aristotle, 6,000 years before the death of Plato. Agathias remarks (ii 24), truthfully, that it is no longer possible to determine with any certainty when he lived and legislated, p. 1040.

6.   These scriptures were traditionally believed to have been revealed in their entirety to Zoroaster. Only 17 hymns, the Gathas, can, however, be attributed to him. Some parts of Avesta, notably some ancients hymns, Yashts, are substantially pre-Zoroastrian in origin. John R. Hinnells, ed. *Dictionary of Religions,* Penguin Books, Ltd., Harmondsworth, England, 1984, p. 57.

7.   Chatterji, J. C. *The Wisdom of the Vedas,* The Theosophical Publishing House, 1973, p. 16.

8.   *Ibid.,* p. 15.

9.   *Ibid.,* p. 17.

10.   *Ibid.,* pp. 18-19.

11.   *Ibid.,* p. 62.

12.   *Ibid.,* p. 68. (During my research of Brahmanism, I found no trace of the caste system, nor the importance of cattle; in fact, at this early date, even cattle were sacrificed. How did the cow become scared? It was quite disappointing to find and follow the distortion of these excellent principles throughout the ages. The existing schools based on these principles seem to me to be bad examples of their originators.)

13.   There is much controversy over the dates of Zoroaster, but the fact that Zoroastrianism proposes a "concept of duality" may suggest that Zoroaster dates prior to the doctrine of Hinduism, and those of the Veda.

14.   Nietszche, the 19th-Century German philosopher, even entitled one of his works "Thus spoke Zarathustra".

15.   Gathas are also known as "Manthras," which means "sacred words" in Zoroastrianism. This could also be the origin of "Mantras" practiced by the Yogis, of which we find no evidence in the doctrines of the Buddha.

16.   Aehner, *Councils of Ancient Sages*, Teachings, p. 25.

17.   This bears similarity to the philosophy of Heraclitus, the Greek philosopher, and we see how Zoroaster has influenced his thinking.

18.   Mithras was a popular God worshiped by citizens of the Roman Empire from the 2nd to the 5th century BCE. He was an Indo-Iranian deity and he was worshiped both in Hinduism and Zoroastrianism. Hinnels, p. 216.

19.   Parrinder, p. 191.

CHAPTER THREE

BUDDHISM

Just this I have taught and do teach,
sorrow and the ending of sorrow.

The Buddha

Buddhism originated in India. The Buddist world, which has included the whole of Asia east of Iran, is divisible philosophically into two main parts: the southern and northern schools of Buddhism. The former preserves its sacred literature in the deed Indian language, Pali, while the latter has its scriptures in Sanskrit, Chinese and Japanese, and Tibetan language. In India, Buddhisim lost its identity one thousand years ago.

Unlike most sages of 6th century B.C. India, who were of the Brahman (priest) caste of Aryan society, Buddha (also known as Siddhartha) belonged to the warrior caste. Brahmanism then held a sort of monopoly in religion, and therefore condemned the Buddha's doctrine as unorthodox. The young prince Buddha is said to have fled into the wilderness, leaving behind his former life of luxury as a prince. After years of meditation, he claimed that *mystical realization of liberation from the mundane life* could be attained by means of *knowledge and compassion*. He claimed one might realize *liberation*, which the Buddhists call *"Nirvana"* (in Sanskrit) or *"Nibbana"* (in Pali).

Doubts exist as to how much of the Buddhism contained in even the oldest of the Buddhist canonical writings was actually the teaching of the historical Buddha. The *Theravada*, the only surviving sect of the Southern School, claims that its Pali Canon contains the original doctrines in words actually spoken by Buddha. However, its books were not committed to writing until the 1st century B.C., *five hundred years* after Buddha began to teach. (These words had been passed down orally through some 15 generations of teachers and pupils in collections of recitations called *sutras* (Sanskrit) or *suttas* (Pali). One can imagine the shifts in individual interpretations, not to mention the many dialect changes, that the original language must have gone through, and the loss that those teachings have suffered in their translations into other languages).

We do not have any proof that Buddha's teachings were recorded during his lifetime. It is possible that some of the doctrines presented five hundred years later were original and it is also possible that they were wholly transformed, since they were handed down orally 15 times. The fact is we do not know how much of the existing doctrines attributed to Buddha are his actual words.

The Bible was also written by the disciples of Jesus and not by Jesus Christ himself. In fact, the only Holy Book that contains the original doctrines of the prophet is the Koran. It is a well-known that the prophet Mohammad himself dictated those doctrines to Hazrat Ali, as he received them inwardly, the words of which were written during his lifetime. This does not mean that the Koran has not been subjected to misunderstanding and misinterpretation. Always, words can be misleading, and in order to understand the doctrines of the prophets, we need to experience those doctrines. To truly understand the doctrines of Buddha, we need to have followed him into the forest and experienced everything that he did and only then we would know and understand what he meant by *knowledge* and *compassion* as the means of liberation. The terms exist on so many different levels. If we have not experienced the "compassion" and "knowledge" that Buddha teaches, those doctrines will be changed and transformed according to our individual the experience.

Like the words *knowledge* and *compassion*, the word *fun* can be used to define experiences that differ with every individual. What one person consider *fun* may be quite the opposite to another. Similarly, when two people look at the same scene, what they perceive is not necessarily the same. Perception is a complex process extending far beyond the mere registration of light, sound, and other impulses from the external world. Perceiving is like solving a puzzle; we piece together assorted clues to form a comprehensive internal picture, and gain an acceptable version of reality. We perceive not only with our eyes, but with the whole person that we are: our past experiences, our present state of mind, our memories, dreams, and desires. *We see what we want to see.* A green, lively garden may seem quite different to a man sentenced to death, who has but an hour to live, than to a prisoner who has a lifetime sentence, a poet, or a child.

Words, especially those representing large concepts such as *knowledge* and *compassion*, oblige us to use our experiences and memories to make sense of them. What I may understand of *passion* will not be the understanding of Buddha, but will be *my* interpretation according to *my* experience. Our understanding of the Scriptures, even if those doctrines were written by the prophet himself, is still limited because we have not experienced their reality. But somehow we have to retrace Buddha's every step to reach the salvation he was pointing to. In order to understand Buddha's doctrines we have to *become Buddha.* We must practice his doctrines, so that they will lead us to true understanding. Buddha represents a stage of awareness and a stage in religion, just like Moses, Christ, and Mohammad.

According to the *dictionary of religions*: "The word Buddha is not a proper name; it denotes a state of being. In the classical language of India it means 'enlightened' or 'awakened,' the state of having direct knowledge of the true nature of things, or truth. 'He who sees the truth sees the Buddha, and he who sees the Buddha sees the truth, is a Buddhist way of expressing it.'"[1]

The prophets of God are *Messengers.* They have brought a Holy Message that must be heard and acted upon, a divine Message, a revelation, a mystical experience of Truth, in complete harmony with their state of being. The Messenger who brings the Message will prepare the way for the wayfarers, the ones who want to set out on the path of self knowledge. He is the Messenger and their guide to the mystical Kingdom of Truth. We read in the Bible:

> Behold, I send my messenger before thy face, Who shall prepare thy way; the voice of one crying in the wilderness: Prepare the way of the Lord, make his paths straight.
>
> (Mark 1:2)

The Messengers of God are not fixed symbols who become heroes after their death and idols to be placed in churches, temples and mosques for worship. Each Messenger represents a stage or a part of self-knowledge, that must be attained and experienced by those who hear them.

According to Buddhist philosophy, the Buddha-nature is of three kinds. The first is dharma-kaya, the pure and absolute essence of Buddha-hood. The second is sambhoga-kaya, the truth in the realm of celestial bliss, the non-mortal realm. The third is nirvana-kaya, the form assumed by Buddha-nature, when a historical manifestation occurs, in the form of human life. One example of such manifestation is Siddhartha Gotama, who lived in India in the 6th century B.C. According to Buddhist thought of all schools there have been many such manifestations in the course of history, and there will be many more, any person who would attain that stage of Buddha-hood. This is true of all prophets and the stages each represent. In the Bible we read: "Where I am you may be also"[2] and in the Koran "I am but a man like any other, I hear the angelic voice."[3]   Both prophets – Jesus Christ representing Christianity and Hazrat Mohammad representing Islam – claim that they are people just like us and where they are we can also be. What we have just said, this human capability, to reach an exalted state of being one which is compatible to the prophets and Messengers of Truth, is perhaps the most important and the most misunderstood doctrine of religion.

However, the Muslim *Mullah* will never accept that it is possible to experience what Hazrat Mohammad did, denies any real relationship with God is possible, and that such an experience by any other than the prophet himself is forbidden by God. The Christian priest's insistence that Jesus Christ is the Son of God is also denying the same possible experiences. But the words of the prophet claim otherwise.

> But to all who received him, who believed in his name, He gave power to become children of God; Who were born not of blood nor of will of the flesh nor of the will of man, but for God.
>
> (John 1:10-14)

In fact we are all the children of God. God has created mankind equally, and all can set foot on the path of self-discovery to find the Truth and to unite with God the merciful or the Father in Heaven.

The message of God to man is "Know Thyself." The Messengers of God represent a certain stage of this total self-awareness that each individual must reach with the help of the one who will show the way.

The first stage is perhaps represented by Zoroaster, for his basic doctrines, "Rightful deed, Rightful thought and Rightful speech," are the first steps towards inner purity, growth, and the acquisition of wisdom. The gates of knowledge will never open unto impure hearts, the great Sufi teacher of the time, Hazrat Salaheddin Ali Nader Angha, explains in the book of his Massnavi:

> The heart totally delivered from impurity,
> Will commence the journey to discovery.

BUDDHA'S DOCTRINE AND THE RESURRECTION OF THE SOUL

After Zoroastrianism, the next page of religion takes us to the doctrines of Buddha and his Message.

Buddha said three characteristics condition life and all that lives, including human beings. These are:

(1)   Impersonality, unsubstantiality.

(2)   Impermanence, change.

(3)   Imperfection, sorrow.

Sorrow is a cornerstone of Buddhist theory. "Just this I have thought and do teach," declared Buddha, "*sorrow, and the ending of sorrow.*"

The Indian-Hindu and Jain, as well as the Buddhist, find life essentially unsatisfactory and imperfect; each recognizes life full of sorrow and pain. Hinayan[4] Buddhism, like other Indian religions, aimed at release from the world of sorrow primarily through *liberation* or *Nibbana.*

The existence of suffering in life, according to Buddha, is the first of the Four Noble Truths, which are:

(1)   That life is subject to sorrow;

(2)   That this sorrow is caused by ignorance, which results in desire-attachment;

(3)   That this sorrow can be eliminated by the elimination of desire-attachment;

(4)   That the way to eliminate desire-attachment is to follow the Eight-fold path.

The sections of the Noble Eight-fold Path are:

(1)   Right Views: Seeing life as it is, in accord with the fundamental Three Characteristics and appreciating the Four Truths;

(2)   Right Mindedness: Being motivated by friendly thoughts, without prejudice, toward one's fellow human beings and toward all other forms of sentient life;

(3)   Right Speech: Speaking kindly and truthfully and narrating incidents accurately;

(4)   Right Action: Acting skillfully and sympathetically while avoiding vain or violent effort;

(5)   Right Livelihood: Practicing a means of living that does not cause oneself or others to infringe on lawful morality;

(6)   Right Endeavor: Self-perfection by avoiding and rejecting ignoble qualities, while acquiring and fostering noble qualities;

(7)   Right Mindfulness: The cultivation and practice of self-awareness and compassion, resulting in self-reliance and equanimity, and;

(8)   Right Concentration: Contemplation culminating in intellectual intuition, and wisdom.

According to the written teachings, a summary of Buddha's philosophy of life is this; in order to attain *Nibbana*, or liberation, we must escape the "wheel of becoming" – the process of birth and death – for this will continue as long as our material desires attach us to the world. What Buddha meant by this has remained very obscure throughout the ages and has caused the greatest misunderstanding of his doctrines, for this message has been misconstrued as "reincarnation." As we define it today, reincarnation means that once a person dies, he is born again into another body and to another set of parents, living the life he deserves according to his actions in the past lifetime; this cycle continues until he becomes pure. However, the life and birth that Buddha describes does not take place within the material world, as is the common belief of the Buddhist and many others who have blindly accepted such a concept as "reincarnation," almost on the basis of childish fantasy. The life and birth in question has little to do with the body and the physical mold; instead, it takes place in the soul. Let us explain this further according to Sufi discipline.

As our consciousness grows and expands, inferior stages of knowledge die, and we are born into a more superior state of inner knowledge. The new life following each death signifies a stage of growth. In the final stage, a person's soul is awakened and is born into *heaven* where he acquires knowledge of the unseen. The desires of his body bind him no longer. Although the body has to be taken care of, he is no longer just a body, but body and soul. In all religious scriptures, *"life"* begins only at this point.[5] This resurrection and awakening should take place during one lifetime and not in infinite numbers and cycles. Once the soul is released from constant flux and change, it is delivered and liberated from its earthly attachments and becomes eternal; death can no longer threaten. This is the resurrection that all the prophets refer to, not a day when all graves spring open and the dead arise. Resurrection is not for dead bones, but for the living soul. One has to rise from the material stage, which means that one's existence no longer depends on or is bound to the material. It is a holy rebirth that takes place in the Kingdom of Heaven as Jesus Christ instructs and must take place before death of the body.

Similarly, a fetus, while in the mother's womb, acquires limbs and organs and all that it needs for life in the material world; and although he does not use them in the womb, he is developing them. He does not need a mouth; his nourishment comes from a different source. He does not need lungs or legs or arms; he is preparing for the next stage in which he will need to live a different life. If the fetus has not developed the right and necessary means of life outside the womb, he cannot return to the womb. He will be incomplete and unable to survive at birth; if he does, he will live an incomplete life.

Whatever is to be achieved is achieved during one's material lifetime. It does not matter what shape your body is or in which environment and under which circumstances or in which country you live, whether you are poor or rich, it makes no difference. The life of Buddha should be evidence enough that even a prince can give up the material for the sake of the soul's liberation. The question is: does one want liberation; does one feel imprisoned by the senses and the limited material world and desire to free himself of worldly and temporary attachments and develop the means for eternal life? If he does, shouldn't seventy years, an average lifetime be long enough? And second, with regards to reincarnation, what seems even more absurd is to think what the spirit of man could attain in the form of an animal! And third, what happens to one's experiences, memories and knowledge, those that one has acquired during one's lifetime?

Perhaps the interpretations of Zen from Buddhism, that translates to the "Sudden Awakening" is more in line with the teachings of the Buddha. Again, in the Massnavi, Ravayeh Hazrat Salaheddin says:

Unaware of the mysteries of the journey to God thou be, The spell of untimely sleep from the friend has stolen thee.

Is it because we do not want to be responsible for our actions, that many of us choose to believe resurrection must wait until after death, or that we shall be born again and again until we become pure. This is a very simple way of looking. It is the least threatening, and does not oblige us to do anything, there is no need to worry as one will just be born again. We seem to have changed the early doctrines of many religions to suit our material desires, to make our lives easier in a superficial way. But no matter how much we try to deny it, the soul, trapped within the body like a bird within a cage, yearns to break free, and we have but one lifetime in which to let it fly. Like a pearl within its shell, the soul shines and waits within us to be discovered, and will never be seen if we do not expend the effort necessary to find it.

It is this misunderstanding of the original doctrines that causes the existing misconceptions referred to earlier; these are the cause of differences between the religions, people are fighting over food they have never tasted. The words and the teachings of the prophets (Zoroaster, Buddha, Moses, Jesus, and Mohammad) are in accordance with one another, but they represent different stages of the liberation of the soul. Misunderstanding between different religions throughout history, still a problem today, are not caused by differences within the original doctrines but by differences of *interpretation*. As we read the New Testament of the Bible:

> Think not that I have come to abolish the law and the prophets; I have come not to abolish them but to fulfill them. For truly, I say to you, till heaven and earth pass away, not a dot will pass from the law until all is accomplished. Whoever then relaxes one of the least of these commandments and teaches men so, shall be called least in the kingdom of heaven; but he who does them and teaches them shall be called great in the Kingdom of Heaven.[6]

Does what we have just read seem like a contradiction or a continuation of the Zoroastrian and Buddhist doctrines we have examined? The Koran of the Muslims also includes these doctrines and many like them, honoring the prophets that have come before and seeking to unite the doctrines in their final stage: *"the Seventh heaven."*[7]

Out of many quotations in the Koran that unite all religions and show similarity between the doctrines, I have chosen the following two:

> Do they seek
> For other than the Religion of God?
> While all creatures
> In the heavens and on earth
> Have, willing or unwilling,
> Bowed to His Will
> And to him shall they
> All be brought back.[8]

> Say, "We believe in God,
> And in what has been revealed to us
> And what was revealed to
> Abraham, Isma'il, Isaac, Jacob, and the Tribes,
> And in (the Books)
> Given to Moses, Jesus, and the prophets,
> From their Lord:
> We make no distinction
> Between one and another among them
> And to God do we bow our will (in Islam).[9]

The liberation of the soul, according to **Islamic Sufism**, is achieved in seven stages; *Islam*, is its final stage. "The mystical realization of liberation from the mundane life," according to Buddha, is only the first stage of this liberation. "Just this I have taught and do teach," declared Buddha, "Sorrow, and the ending of sorrow." This release from the Buddhist world of sorrow is the primary step toward the true knowledge of and unity with God. The prophets who follow Buddha will represent the progressive stages in Nibbana or Nirvana up to the attainment of total liberation.

In the book *Nirvan* which is a description of the journey of man's soul to salvation through different stages, the last stage that is Islam, meaning surrender to Truth, is thus described by the Sufi Master Hazrat Shah Maghsoud: "On the seventh day, man was housed in the Empyrean. A sound of hope echoed in the infinite existence: 'Nonentity is not, and existence is eternal.' Nirvan, who had left the world of appearances, thrust away the dust, lost his identity in the infinite, and regained peace."[10]

Nirvana, according to the Buddhists, derives from *nir-va*, meaning "to bow." Buddhist texts compare the attainment of *Nirvana* to the wind blowing out the flame. While Nirvana can be said to be the annihilation of ignorance and sorrow, Buddhists emphatically deny that *Pari-Nirvana* means annihilation. Mahayanists[11] describe it as *Tathata*, or "suchness," and claim that it cannot even be named "The One," since it is not distinct from anything. Hinayanists equate it with cessation, holding that "the cessation of becoming is *Nibbana*." When urged to speak more, Buddha replied, "No measure measures him who has reached the Goal; by what measure is the immeasurable measured? No words describe the indescribable."

CHAPTER THREE ENDNOTES

1. John R. Hinnells, *Dictionary of Religions*, Penguin Books 1984,. p. 69.

2. John 14:3.

3. Koran S.XVIII. 110.

4. A Sanskrit word made up of two parts: *Hina* (low or inferior) and *Yana* (a vehicle or means of salvation). The combination of these two was applied by a Buddhist school of thought that called itself MAHAYANA, i.e., 'great or superior means of salvation' – superior, that is, to the eighteen other Buddhist schools, Hinnels, p. 148.

5. The notion of being "born again" is also found in Christian doctrine. *"Except a man be born again he cannot see the kingdom of God"* (John 3:3). This rebirth is an awakening, says Paul: *"Awake, thou that sleepest and arise from dead."*

6. Matthew 5:17-19.

7. There are seven stages that the disciple (salek) must pass through before achieving true self-knowledge and cognition of God. These are: seeking, love, knowledge, contempt, unity, wonder, and the finally poverty and annihilation.

8. *Ibid.*, S.III.83. p. 145.

9. *Ibid.*, S.III.84.

10. Shah Maghsoud Sadegh Angha, *Nirvan*, University Press of America, 1986, Lanham MD, 20706, p. 36.

11. Mahayana; a development of thought and practice within Buddhism from about the first century CE. Hinnells, *Dictionary of Religions*, p. 197.

CHAPTER FOUR

BUDDHIST AND HINDU MEDITATION

The gates of heaven will not open on to
those who mortify themselves.

Hazrat Salaheddin Ali Nader Angha

The Buddhist meditation, known as yoga, derives from the understanding of Buddha's doctrines.

Yoga Philosophy

The word *yoga* describes the disciplines for self-development, primarily for the realization of God by direct experience. But *yoga* may also be used for such lesser ends as the control of natural forces and physiological processes. "*Yoga*" comes from the Sanskrit root "*yuj*" meaning "to yoke" the individual self with the Divine. One who practices yoga is called a yogi.

The States of Yoga

The eight successive steps of yoga are given in Sanskrit to emphasize that there are no exact English equivalents to the deeper meanings of these terms, the meanings which are discovered in experience.

(1)   *Yama* is the exclusion of evil actions, that is, self-control.

(2)   *Niyama* is the regular and complete observance of moral rules.

(3)   *Asana* means posture; the most famous is the *"Lotus Posture,"* in which the worshiper sits with feet placed soles up on the opposite thigh.

(4)   Pranayama is the practice of controlled breathing.

(5)   Pratyhara is the restraint of the senses.

(6)   Dharana refers to steadying the mind by intense concentration on a single object.

(7)   Dhyana is deep meditation.

(8)   Samadhi is the attainment of pure consciousness at the highest level of one's being.   The samadhi experience is overwhelming and not definable.

Meditation plays an important part in the practice of Buddhism. It is said to help improve and perfect character and stimulate intuition and wisdom. Buddhist meditation begins with simple breathing exercises; by learning to control one's breathing, one learns to calm and, ultimately, to control the body. With the body under control, the more difficult and important task of controlling the mind follows. With one's thoughts controlled and purified, the character can be perfected; then wisdom and intuition mature, until finally mystical realization is won.

In Buddhist meditation, it is the individual who must change, not the outside world. The wisdom that enables one to accomplish this should not be confused with factual knowledge, such as that acquired by conventional education. Rational thinking and reasoning can be obstacles to wisdom, because attainment is essentially a process of passing beyond the mind. Buddha insisted that knowledge must be tempered with kindness and understanding; neither knowledge nor compassion alone ensures perfection.

In the southern school of Buddhism, the science of meditation has three principle groups of exercises:

(1)   Contemplation of the Four Sublime States of Mind: Benevolence, Compassion, Sympathy, and Equanimity.

(2)   Practice of the Four Applications of Mindfulness: These exercises involve concentration upon one's body, one's sensations, one's states of mind, and one's mental conceptions.

(3)   Absorption in the Material and Immaterial Spheres: The most important exercise of all, this involves contemplation of four material and four immaterial spheres. Meditation on the objects of form results in a state of tranquility within the mind and the senses. Meditation on formless objects involve the contemplation of infinite space, unlimited consciousness, emptiness, and neither perception nor non-perception.

However, although the word yoga means union with the divine and its practice according to the teachings of Buddha should lead to salvation or attaining Nirvana, the programs offered in yoga classes today are mostly of a physical nature, concentrating on the health and beauty of the body through physical exercises and a vegetarian diet. The Yogi is so concerned with what he eats because, strangely, he believes that he becomes what he eats. But the food the spirit or soul needs is not the solid food the body needs for its chemical functions. The food of the soul must be of another kind, one that must be in harmony with the subtle state of the soul.

Some yogis not only eliminate animal protein from their diets but also follow an extreme regimen of near starvation. "The gates of heaven will not open on to those who mortify themselves."[1] Although it is quite admirable and extraordinary how much control they are able to gain over their bodies through severe discipline, this is not the purpose of meditation. The health of the body is very important and one should strive to maintain this through a balanced diet. However, the training and the maintenance of the body alone will not lead one toward Nirvana.

In classes teaching Buddhist meditation, especially *transcendental meditation* (known as *T.M.*), the method of long hours of chanting is used for the purpose of self-discipline and the training of the body and the mind. The given words or phrases, which must be repeated continuously, are called *mantras*. In *Concentration, An Approach to Meditation,* Earnest Wood states, "I have recently read in one of the Upanishads the recommendation that a certain 16-syllabled mantra should be repeated 35 million times, and one commentator offers the calculation that it can be done in twenty years at the rate of about five thousand times each day, or eight times per minute for ten hours!"[2] The idea, according to Earnest Wood is: (1) the words help to keep the mind on the object they refer to, and (2) their repetition or rhythm has an effect on the body.

However, without going to such an extreme to keep the mind fixed upon a word, repeating *mantras* may serve as a technique for concentration as a preparatory step toward meditation. However, I would not use such a concentration technique in my classes, because a word stands as a symbol for a meaning. That the repeated words are of no significance and are repeated for rhythm and effect are not reasons enough for devoting long hours to the task. I find there are so many other techniques of concentration more rewarding and effective than the repetition of meaningless words.

In the spring of 1989, a television program that was broadcasted in San Diego discussing controversial issues regarding T.M. announced that the government of West Germany has issued leaflets as warning of ill effects caused by T.M.

One mantra, however, is supposed to have a meaning: *Om,* meaning "*I am that.*" "It is said that *Om* is a unique word, being composed of *a* plus *u* plus *m*. It begins with *a*, the first articulation we can make in the back of the mouth, goes through the middle sound *u*, and ends with the last sound we can make, *m*. *A*, followed rapidly by *u*. forms *o*, and thus we have *Om*. Thus, *Om* goes from the beginning to the end of all articulate sounds and includes all meanings of unity as well."[3] Historically I have not found any record or evidence of Buddha reciting and repeating mantras. His meditation took place in silence.

However, *manthras*, according to the dictionary of religions, are "sacred words" in Zoroastrianism. Primarily these are the *gathas* of Zoroaster, but the term is also used to refer to all prayers. Mantras exist under the same context in Hinduism. The usage today, however, does not have a religious connotation and a form of prayer, but the utilizing of particular sounds for their effects on the body and concentration, as mentioned earlier by Earnest Wood.

CHAPTER FOUR ENDNOTES

1   Molana Salaheddin Ali Nader Angha, the teacher of the school of Islamic Sufism, Lectures.

2.   Earnest Wood, *Concentration, An Approach to Meditation*, Theosophical Publishing House, Wheaton, Illinois, 1949, p. 123.

3.   *Ibid.*, p. 129.

CHAPTER FIVE

THE SPREAD OF BUDDHISM IN CHINA AND JAPAN

*There is much wisdom and most
important of all is to achieve life.*

Buddhism was introduced to China about A.D. 65, where it was patronized by some emperors, persecuted by others, and flourished in a number of sects. Buddhism penetrated Japan around A.D. 55.

In 1191, the first Zen sect was founded in Japan. (Japanese *Zen-na*, Chinese *Ch'an*, Sanskrit *Dhyana*, Pali *Jhana* – in all four languages, the word means meditation.) The origins of Zen are as much Taoist as Buddhist and, because its flavor is so peculiarly Chinese, it may be best to inquire into its Chinese ancestry.

Three religions have played a major role in China's three thousand years of history. They are Confucianism, Taoism and Buddhism. Confucianism and Taoism are indigenous to China. They had both been in existence for some five hundred years before Buddhism was introduced from India. But even before the rise of Confucianism and Taoism, an earlier religion (from which both Confucianism and Taoism each in its own way grew) had held sway in China for nearly a thousand years. Religion in China had thus a history extending over a millennium and a half before its notions were challenged by a foreign tradition.

So powerful was this indigenous tradition that, after the introduction of Buddhism to China, Buddhism became increasingly Chinese in character.

Purely Chinese schools of Buddhism were born. But again, so influential was the impact of Indian thought and religion upon Chinese minds and philosophy that Confucianism and Taoism also underwent change. Buddhism began to play an increasingly important role in Chinese philosophy. Several schools of Buddhism were brought to China from India, and several more were developed by the Chinese. In all, there were some thirteen major schools originating from Buddhism. The most significant Chinese contribution was the Ch'an school. While originating in certain teachings of Buddha, Ch'an was, for the most part, the philosophic-religious creation: Buddhism with a distinctly Taoist accent. As a part of Chinese philosophy, the Ch'an school transformed Buddhism to a simpler and more practical form. The Chinese approach to Buddhism stresses the doctrine of universal over individual salvation. Historically, Zen may be regarded as the fulfillment of long traditions of Indian and Chinese culture, but it is actually much more Chinese than Indian.

Since the 12th century, Zen Buddhism has rooted itself deeply and most creatively in the culture of Japan, as the fruition of all three great cultures and as a unique and peculiarly instructive example of a way to liberation. However, as we are about to see, by the time it reaches Japan, Zen Buddhism has shifted a long way from its true source, the magnificent and powerful doctrines of the Veda, at the core of Hinduism.

Zen Buddhism

The Zen understanding of the doctrines of Buddha differs somewhat from India's, mainly because of the simpler approach of Zen. "What is Zen? This is one of the most difficult questions to answer," says Daisetz Teitaro Suzuki,[1] the greatest authority on Zen Buddhism. The significance of Zen, according to Suzuki, evades all definition and explanation. Zen can not be converted into ideas and can never be described in logical terms.

Zen practice is derived from the *awakening experience of Buddha*, which took place suddenly one night as he sat under the Bodhi Tree at Gaya after seven years of meditation in the forest. This event is the height of Zen, and all verbal doctrine is secondary to the wordless transmission of the experience itself. Buddha is said to have transmitted this awakening to his chief disciple, Mahakasyapa, by holding up a flower and remaining silent. "Thus from the standpoint of Zen," says Alan Watts, "Buddha never spoke a word," despite the volumes of scriptures attributed to him. Buddha's real message always remained unspoken because words could never explain them."[2] Zen has a famous saying:

> Those who know do not speak;
> those who speak do not know.[3]

This "noble silence," along with the Four Noble Truths (listed in ch. 4), summarize Buddha's doctrines according to Zen practitioners. Zen mistrusts the intellect and does not rely on traditional methods of reasoning. Zen suggests a new point of view; seeing conventional ways of thinking as a kind of slavery, Zen masters urge us to break away from logic. To the Zen practitioners there is no logic in the actual living of life, for life is superior to logic. "*A flower is not red, nor is the willow green.*"[4]

Zen awakening occurs immediately and instantaneously without passing through preparatory stages. Nirvana cannot be approached by stages, by the slow process of the accumulation of knowledge, but must be realized in a single flash of insight; in Japanese, the word of the experience is *satori*, "sudden awakening." Zen emphasizes immediacy and naturalness:

> No thought, no reflection, no analysis
> No cultivation, no intention,
> let it settle itself.[5]

Zen communication is always "direct pointing":

> Outside teaching; apart from tradition.
> Not founded on words and letters.
> Pointing directly to the human mind.
> Seeing into one's nature and attaining Buddhahood.[6]

The practice of Zen, however, is not a means to the end of awakening. The practice of Zen is not the true practice as long as it has an end in view, because to practice with an end in view is to have one eye on the practice and the other on the end, indicating lack of concentration and lack of sincerity. Zen practitioners claim that one does not practice Zen to become a Buddha. One practices it because one is a Buddha from the beginning and this *original realization* is the starting point of Zen life.[7]

Zen experience does not imply any specific course of action, but turns without hesitation to anything that presents itself to be a state of mind functioning without blocks, conflicts, or alternatives. Much of Zen training consists of confronting the dilemmas the student must learn to handle without stopping to deliberate and choose. The response to the situation must follow with the immediacy of sound issuing from the hands when they are clapped or of sparks from a match when struck. These are called koans. Koans are puzzles or questions, which are intentionally misleading.

> Koans as a whole are called *wisteria vines* or *entanglements* and particular groups are *cunning barriers* (kikan) and *hard to penetrate* (nanto). A Zen student does not really know Zen unless he discovers it for himself. The Chinese proverb, "What comes in through the gate is not family treasure," is understood in Zen to mean that what someone else tells you is not your own knowledge. *Satori* comes only after one has exhausted one's thinking, only when one is convinced that the mind cannot grasp itself.
> The basic position of Zen is that *it has nothing to say, nothing to teach*, because the truth of Buddhism is so self-evident that it is, if anything, concealed by explaining it. Therefore, the master does not "help" the student in any way, since helping would actually be hindering. On the contrary, he goes out of his way to put obstacles and barriers in the student's path.
> The preliminary koan begins, therefore, to obstruct the student by sending him off in the direction exactly opposite from that in which he should look. The student is, in fact, encouraged to make a total fool of himself, to whirl around and around like a dog trying to catch up with its own tail.[8]

Meditation Hall

The Western student might be startled by monastic Zen as it exists today in Japan. He will find that Zen is enforced with the big stick, involving a disciplinary regimen somewhat similar to the old-fashioned British public school system.

> Much importance is attached to the physical posture of Za-zen. The monks sit on firmly padded cushions with legs crossed and feet soles-upward upon the thighs. The hands rest upon the lap, and left over the right, with palms upward, and thumbs touching one another. The body is held erect, and the eyes are left open so that their gaze falls upon the floor a few feet ahead.

> While monks are thus seated, two attendants walk slowly back and forth along the floor between the platforms, each carrying a 'warning stick.' As soon as they see a monk

going to sleep or sitting in an incorrect posture, they stop before him and beat him on the shoulders.[9]

The usual first koan is called: *Original Face*. At first, the student is told to discover his *Original Face*, as it was before his father and mother conceived him. He is told to return when he has discovered it, and to give some proof of discovery. In the meantime, he is under no circumstances to discuss the problem with others or to seek their help. As soon as he is told how to sit by the *head monk*, he starts to seek the proper view of his koan. Pondering the problem of his *Original Face*, he tries and tries to imagine what he was before he was born, or, for that matter, what he now is at the very center of his being, what is the basic reality of his existence apart from his extension in time and space.

He soon discovers that the teacher has no patience whatever with philosophical or other wordy answers. He wants to be shown. He wants something concrete, some solid proof. The student therefore starts to produce such "specimens of reality" as lumps of rock, leaves, and branches, shouts, gestures of the hands – anything and everything he can imagine. But all is resolutely rejected until the student, unable to imagine anything more, reaches the conclusion finally that he does not know.

At this stage, the student is now ready to begin his Zen training in earnest. It is not quite the paradox it seems to say that Zen training can begin only when it has been finished. For this is the basic principle, that awakening is not truly attained unless it also implies the life of Buddhahood, the manifestation of the *marvelous use of Void*.

At this point, the teacher begins to present the student with koans that ask for impossible feats of action or judgment.

"Stop the ship on the distant ocean. Take the four divisions of Tokyo out of your sleeve."[10]

Zen is just a trick of words; as with the principle of extracting a thorn with a thorn, Zen is extricating people from the tangle in which they have landed themselves by confusing words with ideas and reality.

"The continued practice of Za-Zen now provides the student with a clear, unobstructed mind into which he can toss the koan like a pebble into a pool and simply watch to see what his mind does with it.

As the work goes on, crucial koan alternate with subsidiary koan, which explore the implication of the former, and give the student a thorough working acquaintance with every theme in the Buddhist view of the universe, presenting the whole body of understanding in such a way that he knows it in his bones and nerves. By such means, he learns to respond with it instantly and unwaveringly in the situations of everyday life.[11]

Finally, this energetic use of koan can be considered as a means of exhausting the strength of egoistic will. "Awakening is to know what reality is not. It is to cease identifying oneself with any object of knowledge whatsoever. Just as every assertion about the basic substance or energy or reality must be meaningless, any assertion as to what *I am* at the very roots of my being must also be the height of folly."[12]

The following poem translated from "Ikkyu's Doka," The Young East, says:

> We eat, excrete, sleep, and get up;
> This is our world.
> All we have to do after that –
> is to die.[13]

Some Zen opponents find the discipline too vigorous and on the extreme side. Others argue that to become free from the confines of logic may be a good idea for one who lives in a monastery, but how could this principle be applied to our day-to day living in a city, where one is continuously faced with challenges and is obliged to make decisions? In addition, how can one be absolutely sure, once one lets go of logic, that the state of wandering mind in the Void may be a healthy one? a person who merely wanders in the street may be in such a state, like a boat drifting aimlessly upon the water but that is impractical or undesirable for most of us. How worthy is a principle that cannot be applied to everyday life.

Others who turn to Zen and other such disciplines for the purpose of self-discovery and direction in life, find Zen is incapable of answering their most important questions: "Who am I," and "What is the purpose of life?" They are disappointed to find that Zen offers no goal at all and claims that "What I am at the roots of my being is the height of folly to want to find out."

I look at Zen as an interesting technique for realizing that in the face of the absolute existence, one is ignorant; that neither logic nor reasoning can explain, for example, one's Original Face, what one was before conception. The stage of reaching one's ignorance and understanding the limits of our logic and reasoning is a very important stage in itself. But when one exhausts one's mental and reasoning power, what then? Is knowledge impossible? To arrive at ignorance is fine, but it cannot be an end. In fact, realizing that one does not know is perhaps an early stage (perhaps the first stage) toward knowledge. When ignorance is reached it must then be replaced by knowledge, the same way the emptiness and the state of Void must be replaced. The mind cannot stay in a state of Void. Zen has a lack of purpose and seems incomplete and in need of much explanation.

Sufism teaches that life is full of *love, beauty, and hope.* There is much wisdom and knowledge to achieve, and most important of all is to achieve LIFE. We do not need to retreat from the world, because it is not sorrowful or pitiful, yet we need to find a definite goal in life and cast some light upon the darkness of confusion and aimless wandering. The flight of Buddha into the wilderness was a symbol of forsaking life's temporary pleasures in order to seek Eternal Bliss and Eternal Life; unfortunately, his action has been taken too literally through the ages. It is not unusual to find many Buddhist 'retreat centers' high up in the mountains, as are convents and monasteries. But instead of retreating from the world, we need to understand that it is passing, that we cannot become attached to it and settle eternally in it. The material world is but a road on which we are passing. Surely as we will leave all our desires and treasures behind, is it not best to detach ourselves from worldly treasures and try to acquire that which we can keep forever? Does not hiding from the world give away our weakness to temptation?

The eminent Imam of Islam, Hazrat Ali, explains this in *Nahjul-Balagha*:

> Verily this world is a house of truth for those who look into it deeply and carefully, an abode of peace and rest for those who understand its ways and moods, and it is the best working ground for those who want to procure rewards for life hereafter. It is a place of acquiring knowledge and wisdom for those who want to acquire them, a place of worship for friends of God and angels. It is the place where Prophets receive revelations of the Lord. It is the place for virtuous people and saints to do good deeds and to be assigned rewards for the same; only in this world they could trade with God's Favors and Blessings and only while living here they could barter their good deeds, with His Blessing and Reward. Where else could all this be done?[14]

Strength lies not in hiding from the temptations of the material world, but in understanding and withstanding them. Solitude is thus explained by

Hazrat Mir Ghotbeddin Mohammad Angha: "The sanctuary of man is his heart, and that is where he should take refuge. This does not mean that he should separate himself from the society, but that he should live amongst all men but not to partake of their bad habits. This is what the Sufis call *solitude*. For an individual may sit alone but be engaged in numerous thoughts. Such a person is not called solitary."[15]

The wilderness to which one must retreat is within the heart, thus detaching oneself from the heavy loads and bonds of earthly desires and attachments. The Sufi believes in comfort but not in ownership. Things are for him to use, and to make his life more comfortable, those things belong to him, and not the other way around, he does not belong to things.

Once the great Sufi Master Hazrat Shah Maghsoud said to me: "I do not feel an ownership even toward this shirt on my back!" The seeker of eternity is after the eternal and everlasting. He knows that not every yellow metal that shines is gold, thus distinguishing the real from the false, and is never tempted by the false. His treasures are stored elsewhere. According to the teachings of Jesus,

> Do not lay up for yourselves treasures on earth, where moth and rust consume and where thieves break in and steal, but lay up for yourselves treasures in heaven. For where your treasure is, there will your heart be also.
>
> (Matthew 7:19-21)

How can we appreciate light? Only when we have experienced darkness can we appreciate and know *light*.

> The Light of truth shines through the pinhole of hearts, but hearts are beset with transient temptations and desires.[16]

CHAPTER FIVE ENDNOTES

1.   D. T. Suzuki, *Essays in Zen Buddhism*, Grove Press Inc., 196 West Houston St., New York, NY, 10014 1985, p. 267.

2.   Alan W. Watts, *The Way of Zen*, Random House, New York, 1957, p. 45.

3.   *Ibid.*, p. 77.

4.   Suzuki, p. 272

5.   Watts, p. 79.

6.   *Ibid.*, p. 88.

7.   *Ibid.*, p. 154.

8.   *Ibid.*, pp. 163-4.

9.   *Ibid.*, pp. 156-7.

10.   *Ibid.*, pp. 164-6.

11.   *Ibid.*, p. 167.

12.   *Ibid.*, p. 171.

13.   *Ibid.*, p. 162.

14.   Hazrat Ali, Seyed Jafery, trans., *Nahjul Balagha*, Elmhurst, New York, 1978, saying 130, p. 207.

15.   Hazrat Mir Ghotbeddin Mohammad Angha, 40th Sufi Master of Oveyssi School of Sufism, *The Light of Salvation*, University Press of America Inc., 1978, p. 84.

16.   Hazrat Shah Maghsoud Sadegh Angha, *The Message from the Soul*, University Press of America Inc., 1986, p. 39.

CHAPTER SIX

JUDAISM AND CHRISTIANITY

For God alone my soul waits in silence.

The Holy Bible (Psalm 62:1)

The history of religion can be used as a metaphor for every soul's journey toward self-discovery. Buddha's path is only the first step on the way to truth. When Buddha talks of suffering, he is pointing not to life itself, but to the bondage of desires and attachments that cause suffering. His abandonment of wealth and rank liberated him from those attachments, from lust and endless desires; thus he reached the stage he called *freedom*. But what comes after the abandonment of physical attachment? Judaism takes us farther along the path. Freed from worldly attachments, the soul thirsts for knowledge.

Judaism gave us, for the first time in religious history, direct instruction and guidance from God. God spoke with Moses, and Moses spoke with Him. Moses went to his wandering people with the message of the *Promised Land*, giving them direction to follow. Direct guidance from God is the stage that follows the aimless wandering, the void and emptiness of Buddhism covered in previous chapters.

The Lord also gave Moses instructions to build the temple of worship. When Moses' rebellious people preferred to worship idols made of gold, God gave Moses the *Ten Commandments* to bring down to them.

> Then, as God finished speaking with Moses on Mount Sinai, he gave him the two tablets of stone on which the Ten Commandments were written with the finger of God.
>
> (Exodus 31:18)
>
> Mediate upon all the laws I have given you today, and pass them on to your children. These laws are not mere words; they are your life.
>
> (Deuteronomy 32:46)

The religion of Moses, for the most part, remained among the Jews as words and theory only. The commandments of God announced by Moses remained on stone for they were only heard, never contemplated nor acted upon. Those laws were turned into many traditions, and were passed on from generation to generation and their reality was lost among traditional ceremonies.

> God never revealed his face to Moses, saying,
> You may not see the glory of my face, for man may not see me and live.
>
> (Exodus 33:21)

To witness God at this stage, *Judaism*, is not possible. Later, Jesus Christ comes with the message that it *is* possible to witness God, but only after a spiritual rebirth, which he explained in his preaching.

> Except a man be born again, he cannot see the kingdom of God.
>
> (John 3:3)

With the next stage of religion and spiritual growth comes Jesus Christ, who points to the heart of man and calls it *heaven*. "Seek first the kingdom of God," he taught. This time, the temple of worship was to be found within; no longer was it in the tabernacle made of wood. The commandments, first written on stone, were now to be written in hearts. According to the teachings of Jesus Christ the place of worship, as well as the kingdom of heaven, is nowhere but within.

> And when he was demanded of the Pharisees, when the kingdom of God should come, he answered them and said, the kingdom of God cometh not with observation. Neither shall they say, Lo here! or Lo there! for, behold, the kingdom of God is within you.
>
> (Luke 17:20-21)

Jesus spoke of God as "His Father in heaven," saying that each of us can make direct contact with God through him, Christ the Savior.

No one knows the Father except the Son and anyone to whom
the Son wishes to reveal him.

(Matthew 11:28)

And Jesus insists on inner transformation via meditation through the
temple within the heart.

Do you not know that you are God's temple and that God's
spirit dwells in you?...For God's temple is holy and that temple
you are.

(Corinthians 3:16-17)

Throughout the whole Judeo-Christian tradition the temple is the
place where man goes to worship the Lord who dwells in the innermost
chamber. The real significance of the temple, as was mentioned, is not a
physical building or a place of worship, but the temple within each person.

The God who made the world and everything in it, being Lord
of heaven and earth, does not live in shrines made by man, nor
is he served by human hands, as though he needed anything
since he himself gives to all men life and breath and
everything...He is not far from each one of us.

(Acts 17:24-28)

When you pray, go into your room and shut the door and pray
to your Father who is in secret.

(Matthew 6:6)

Scriptural witness to meditation, however, pervades both the Old testament
and the Gospels. For instance, the Psalms read:

For God alone my soul waits in silence.

(Psalm 62:1)

I commune with my heart in the night; I meditate and search
my spirit.

(Psalm 77:6)

Let my words of my mouth and the meditation of my heart be
acceptable in thy sight. O Lord, my rock and my redeemer.

(Psalm 19:14)

May my meditation be pleasing to him, for I rejoice in the
Lord.

(Psalm 104:34)

Originally, Christian teachings (before they became externalized and
dogmatized by various Christian institutions) focused on awakening from
sleep through the light shed by inner wisdom.

Awake, thou that sleepest and arise from the dead.

Jesus Christ gives the message,

Knock and the door will be opened.

(Ephesians 5:14)

The realm lying behind the door is yet another stage represented by the Messenger that proceeds Jesus Christ; the key to the door, however, is in the holy hands of Mohammad, the prophet of Islam. It is only after entering the temple within, that one is reborn and thus acquires eternal knowledge.

The Koran says:

Do they not travel through the land, so that their hearts may thus learn wisdom; and their ears may thus learn to hear?

Truly it is not their eyes that are blind, but their Hearts which are in their breasts.

(Surah XXII 48)

And God knows all that is in your hearts.

(Koran XXXIII 51)

It is He who sent down Tranquility into Hearts.

(Koran 48:5)

Beyond the limited understanding of the senses, we have a goal and that goal is unity with our identity, the God within. The Sufis speak of the bliss that lies within the heart of man, a bliss that can never be acquired by the mind and grasped by anything other than the heart. Realization of this bliss brings fulfillment and wisdom, and is only achieved through the true practice of religion, which is self-knowledge through meditation.

Let me know myself, Lord, and I shall know thee.

(St. Augustine)

No one can be saved without self-knowledge.

(St. Bernard)

The above quotations reveal that in the long line of Christian sages during the first few centuries A.D., the practice of meditation was more essential than verbal prayer and was practiced regularly in the monasteries. However, like Judaism, Christianity has also become lost in tradition and religious ceremonies, and self-knowledge is no longer an issue, although the meditative tradition at one time dominated early Christianity in the Middle East. St. Anthony established a school of systematic meditation in A.D. 310, on a mountain now called St. Anthony, 65 miles south of Cairo.

Another monastery, the monastery of Tabenna in upper Egypt, was founded by Paul in A.D. 300. In all, there were approximately five thousand monks practicing meditation and austerity in the desert of Nitra, or the Nitron Valley in Egypt, around that time. During the second half of the fourth century, a large number of ascetics lived near Cairo. Christianity began to replace the myths and gods of Egypt, and the sign of the cross was often seen instead of the ancient symbols.[1]

Unfortunately, in spite of the meditations of Jesus and the importance of meditation given in his teachings, Western Christianity has never seriously absorbed the genuine meditative tradition.

However, meditation is the true practice and experience of religion. Religion has one Message: "Know thyself." As I suggested earlier, there is only one religion and only one God according to the doctrines of Islamic Sufism. Yet the different stages of understanding and acquiring the goal of religion, *Know thyself*, are Zoroastrianism, Buddhism, Judaism, Christianity, and Islam. The reason for the existence of different opinions and interpretations of religion and faith is because the actual experience of Truth is missing. That experience is meditation.

If the theory of religion were combined with the practice and with the help of the right guide or teacher, there would be no such confusion. No great teacher of man ever spoke strictly as a theorist; each gave the message of his own experience. Theoretical knowledge alone is like a rose without the scent, like words on a menu instead of food on a plate.

In response to a learned man who asked Abu-Hanifa, *What shall I do now?*, he replied, *Practice what you have learned, for theory without practice is like a body without spirit.*[2] There is no knowledge without action, since knowledge is the product of action and is brought forth and developed and made profitable by the blessings of action. The two things cannot be divorced in any way, just as the light of the sun cannot be separated from the sun itself. Therefore, what words describe in the most beautiful poetical scriptures remains to be discovered by us through meditation.

The difference between knowledge and wisdom in religion is that wisdom is born of experience gained by applied knowledge. Therefore, as important as the theory of religion is, theory alone is worthless. Our goal is to find the wisdom that lies hidden in the heart, and theory alone will not lead us there.

The difference between religion and theology is that theology is merely a system of speculation of the unseen, whereas *religion is experience.*

The artist's ideal is beauty, the scientist's is truth, and the moralist's is goodness. Religion combines all three and wants to make us aware of unity.

Every creative act in science, art, or religion involves a new innocence of perception liberated from the contract of accepted beliefs. In this spirit of innocence, the true scientist looks at the world with young eyes, as if he were seeing it for the first time. He is delighted if this new vision opens the way to a theory or a discovery that upsets the very laws of science on which he has been raised.

The most vital religion would be one that had no creed at all, but that encouraged its believer to seek the truth with all his heart and soul and mind, and to report these truths so that all may benefit, as a scientist does with his discoveries. What a religious flowering we would have! However, this will only take place if we break away from the prejudices we have formed and open ourselves to the truth.

In the succeeding chapters, Part Two, we will be concerned with *self-healing* and how we can use meditation in our day-to-day life, and what actually happens when we meditate. The crucial goal of the next few chapters is to learn how to cope with stress via meditation.

CHAPTER SIX ENDNOTES

1.   Rev. Lawrence Bouldin, et al., *Meditation in Christianity*, Himalaya Publishers, Honesdale, Pennsylvania, p. 7.

2.   Ali Bin Uthman, *Kashf-Al-Mahjub*, translated by Reynold A. Niholson, Islamic Book Foundation, Samanabad, Lahore, 1976, p. 95.

PART TWO

CHAPTER SEVEN

STRESS

Man lives alone, and along the path of life a stranger he is to all, even to the moments of his own life. In this journey without return, the sorrow of desires will wither the freshness of his face as he takes steps towards the unknown, pledged between his past and future searching for the lost songs long hidden in his soul.

Hazrat Shah Maghsoud Sadegh Angha

In the previous chapters the close relationship between religion and the state of meditation was explained. Again, behind the empty words and habitual traditions there existed a message preached by all the Prophets: "Know thyself." This truth, hidden or even lost among so many ornaments, was brought to the light.

Self-awareness, the superior goal of religion, is a journey within, which starts with awakening and hearing the *message of love* through the heart. This takes place by means of meditation. At that time one is able to ascend the ladder of spiritual perfection that finally leads to self-awareness.

"Open your hidden eyes and come, return to the root of the root of your own self,"[2] says Jalal al-Din Rumi, the great Persian Sufi poet. "When you will hear the voice of a friend on that lonely night, you will be delivered from the striking of the serpents and the fear of ants."[3] The words "serpents and ants," common in Persian literature, refer to the mortality of the body and represent a rather morbid but descriptive image of the body being consumed by animals. Man lives in constant fear of such an end, and yet surrenders himself to the world around him and to the rule of the jungle.

"What is man?" asks Nietzsche, "A knot of savage serpents that are seldom at peace among themselves – thus they go forth alone and seek prey in the world."[4]

First let's try to define man. Who is man? What are his abilities and potentials? Science describes man in terms of his physiology with a chemical perspective, but would that be a true definition? Who is man? The cousin of apes evolved from primal ooze to superman or a being unique in cosmic history? The dweller in Plato's cave, or the witness of divine visions? Who is man? The inventor of war? Or the prince of peace? Judas or Jesus?

How can we know what man is? How can we discover the "mystery of humanity"? We may be able to discover our true nature, and the purpose of life, even all the mysteries unknown to us, not by escaping from the finite and relative world but by a complete acceptance of its limitations. Paradoxical as it seems, we search for the meaning of life only when we have seen that it is without purpose: we search for and discover the mystery of humanity only when we are convinced that we know nothing about it at all.

> The wise knows that he does not know,
> The foolish does not.
> Those aware of their poverty shall receive riches,
> And those aware of their loss shall seek and find.[5]

The reason why the materialist and the relativist fail to reach this point is because they use limited tools to try to discover the unlimited reality of man. As a result of trying to measure the ocean with the help of a spoon, they soon abandon faith and openness, and allow their minds to harden into doctrine.

The man who has been created in the *image of God* is today the helpless victim of stress. Quite unaware of his natural resources and unable to reach them, he uses a certain amount of adaptive energy he has to confront the modern everyday conflicts. Why is he so ignorant of his natural resources and the potential that lies within him? How can he reach that source and relieve himself at last of stress?

The recognition of man's potential, the natural energy supply he is connected to, and its activation and assembly through meditation will fortify and enable him to take part in his own fate, creating an environment desirable to himself and to those who surround him. This and more will be the subject of the succeeding chapters that explain "self-healing," an effective stress management technique. The Sufi believes: "Man is the architect of his own environment."[6]

The social and economic structure of modern life has created more stress today than ever before in human history. Burdens are sometimes just too great to bear, and yet some feel they have no other choice but to accept them on a daily basis simply as a fixed component about which they can do little.

Let us consider some general sources of stress (or stressors, as psychologists call it). Environmental stressors include air, noise pollution, and overcrowded living conditions. Other stressors are the constant sense of time urgency, deadline pressures on the job, the feeling of almost always running out of time, that twenty-four hours in one day is just not sufficient. Other psychological stressors are the sense of competition at work or at home, a need to prove oneself all the time, or having to deal with difficult relationships that may involve a problem child, a mate, a friend, or a boss. In fact every small task, such as having to go to the gas station or the market and having to wait in long lines or deal with traffic, are but a few stressors that one might have to face on a daily basis.

While stress has always been a basic part of human life, lifestyles have changed considerably during the last two centuries and are no longer as simple.

"Think about this picture," says Dr. Jackie Swartz.

People slept beneath homemade quilts, awakening naturally at the first sounds of morning, rising with the dawn. They dressed simply in preparation for their day's work in clothes made of natural fibers, perhaps homespun. They had definite jobs to do, maybe the same work their parents had done before them. Their food was homegrown, and if they didn't grow all their food themselves, they bartered with a neighbor, perhaps swapping eggs for corn. Older and younger family members lived together, and children had a feeling of security and identity. There was a lot of caring expressed between the generations. There weren't any telephones or automobiles, and timepieces were scarce. And, of course, there weren't many interruptions in their lives; their days were relatively predictable. Everyone worked hard because heavy physical labor was often a necessary part of their work. A lot of physical exercise, like chopping wood and beating rugs, was a regular part of their lives. At the end of the day, their work was done. Because fuel was regarded as a precious commodity, they went to bed not long after sunset. They slept soundly, naturally, restoring their bodies. Others didn't expect any more of them. Certainly, life was far from perfect then. But there were fewer sources of stress, and people were better equipped to handle the stress that is a part of everyday life.

Contrast this scene with life today. Now, most people are packed into densely populated areas, living and sleeping scant yards from others they don't even know. They are awakened by a mechanical alarm, the first of many mechanical devices that influence or even govern their daily lives. They dress in clothes that are usually made of synthetic materials. Breakfast is often something out of a package, washed down with instant coffee and imitation orange juice. Then they either hop into a metal and glass 'isolation tank' or cram into a subway, bus, or commuter train to be transported to work, which is often far from where they live. This daily ritual stirs their competitive and survival senses as they struggle through heavy traffic or contend with crowds of others heading for work. By this time they're fighting the clock, fighting for their own safety zone, alert to dangers that may slow them down or impinge on their space.[7]

Because of the development of technology, men and women are bombarded with many stressors. As life in big cities becomes faster and more complicated, human beings find themselves under a lot of pressure as they try to adjust. At work, they have to function as fast and efficiently as machinery, and often without any rest. At home, the fast and efficient computer-like character has to become soft, tender and loving in order to meet the needs of loved ones. One may feel the need to be an understanding spouse, a loving parent, or an ideal daughter or son, and as a result be left with no time for oneself to rest from the pressures of the day. Instead, the remaining time may be spent in front of the television, watching mindless adventure shows full of crime and violence, followed by the generally distressing news program in which news of childabuse, homicide, crime, incurable diseases, worldwide social and political uncertainties and turmoil that one can not do anything about are reported. With no other choice but the acceptance of one's feeling of helplessness and hopelessness, the day is over and one retires to bed. Even though our energy level stays the same, because most people do not know how to raise it, the negative effect of stressors are dramatically increased.

While the family unit was strong thirty years ago, a common modern stressor is the breakup of the family and, consequently, the pressures of single parenting. Another stressor is the present relationship between men and women. Instead of acting together as partners and companions, they are in competition for rights, a circumstance that leads not only to individualism but to the necessity of bearing of pressures alone. Having to cope with so much stress in a society that is geared toward individualism rather than toward the establishment of family ties and family bonds requires a level of strength that not every individual has.

In 1986, the American Association for Counseling and Development held a convention in downtown Los Angeles where I was conducting a stress workshop. At the convention I also attended a lecture given by Alex Haley, the author of *Roots*. Haley emphasized "the importance of preserving family bonds and the importance of grandparents to grandchildren." It is evident, however, that the lack of love, attention, and support in the lives of so many people who come from 'broken homes' causes much suffering, and forces many to seek outside help and relief. Such a lack of a sense of belonging may explain why people choose to join groups such as the cult of Jim Jones, where the members were robbed not only of wealth but of life, or why they may seek temporary relief in drugs and alcohol.

Four major stress-related disorders that have recently become especially prominent in the U.S., Western Europe, and Japan according to the latest research are cardiovascular diseases, cancer, arthritis, and respiratory diseases. These are described as the afflictions of civilization that are most prevalent in the sophisticated, developed areas of the world. Diet, environmental contamination, and especially the increased psychosocial stress of post-industrial societies are considered major contributing factors in their development.

Most standard medical textbooks attribute anywhere from 50 to 80 percent of all disease to psychosomatic or stress-related origins. Another alarming statistic is that 30 million Americans suffer from stress-related sleep-onset insomnia.

The most common negative stress reactions serve as early warning signs of damage to the body. They include tightness in the chest, rapid or pounding heartbeat, irritability, difficulty in falling asleep, lack of concentration, forgetfulness, upset stomach, tightness in the neck and shoulders, nagging headaches, dry mouth, sweaty palms, clenched jaws, back pain and pain in other areas in the body that are more vulnerable to stress. Exposure to stressors focuses the stress on the body, so that the muscles contract and become very tense, causing pain and discomfort and a constant feeling of exhaustion. In this state, when faced with a crisis, one is not able to think clearly but tends to panic instead.

As stress continues to build, more damage signs appear: lack of patience, constant stomach pains, thumping heart sounds, and increased smoking or drinking. As the effects of stress accumulate over long periods, negative stress eventually depletes one's supply of adaptive energy. The usual outcome is illness, including migraine headaches, ulcers, high blood pressure, alcoholism, drug addiction, asthma and heart disease.

> Experiments have shown that experimentally induced psychological stress may 'tax' the heart and circulatory system, may decrease the clotting time of the blood, inhibit certain aspects of the immune response, disturb gastric conditions, and cause urinary difficulties, sexual dysfunction, and hormonal problems. Both the acute alarm reaction and the more prolonged stress reaction may contribute significantly to the development and course of mental illness.[8]

Stress reactions, even violent ones, can occur anywhere from 10 to 50 times a day. Medical theory suggests that excessive stress and consequent anxiety play a leading role in disease and emotional illness. Statistics have identified the overwhelming cost of treating stress; the high cost is because the medical profession has a hard time defining the cause of stress. In the few cases when the cause is discovered, it is not obvious that there is anything to be done, and procedures are very costly and frustrating.

Stress is not synonymous with anxiety or tension. Anxiety is a fear reaction to some unknown cause; it is often our body's first response to any sudden change. Tension, on the other hand, is the contraction of tightening of the muscles, either voluntarily or involuntarily.

Emotional responses to fear, anger, and worry are linked to the physical reactions we associate with stress. Some stressors are positive; an example of a positive stressor may be preparing for a marriage. A negative stressor is a death in the family, for example. In each case, we have to do a lot of adjusting. Simply when we are labeling a situation as a "problem," we are in fact producing for ourselves an unpleasant stressor. Each time we react to a stressor, pleasant or unpleasant, we are adapting to some change. Therefore stress is the sum of the adaptive changes that our body makes to help us adjust to various social or environmental situations. It is analogous to temperature change; we respond to heat as we respond to cold. In the same way, we respond to positive demands as well as negative ones.

Hans Selye, an authority on stress, explains how his discovery of stress arose from a very simple set of observations.

> As a medical student, he noted that people show a characteristic fatigue and general discomfort when they are sick; in addition, this general state may arise not only during illness but also after any demanding physical or emotional event. Intrigued by these early observations, Selye began research to identify this consistent physiological response to demanding circumstances.
> He found that a sudden change in temperature, a bacterial infection, a loud noise or a great surprise can all trigger the same system of bodily defenses. Selye called this non-specific reaction to any demanding circumstance stress. Whenever an event triggers this reaction, that event may be termed a stressor. The General Adaptation Syndrome (G.A.S.), Selye's medical term for stress, develops in three stages: the alarm reaction, the stage of resistance, and the stage of exhaustion. The initial alarm reaction is generated by the sympathetic and parasympathetic systems working together. These subsystems adjust bodily functions to meet the stressor. The sympathetic system stimulates the adrenal glands to produce adrenaline. Simultaneously the hypothalamus activates a pattern of hormone release from the pituitary gland. Through its hormonal signals, this master gland regulates the general somatic defenses of the adaptation reaction. In resisting disease or real dangers, these operations are life-saving. During the second phase of G.A.S., certain of the body's neural and endocrine reactions persist until the stressful situation has abated.

The expenditure of energy and vital bodily resources in the first two stages then leads to the third phase of G.A.S., the exhaustion of the individual. This fatigue persists until the body can gain deep rest and replenish itself. If the body does not receive rest sufficient to restore its equilibrium, stress becomes a chronic condition that gradually destroys physical and emotional well-being.

Not only physical stressors but also strong emotions can increase adrenaline production. The organism experiences this state of alarm as preparedness for fight or flight. Although the behavioral components of the fight or flight syndrome may be suppressed or modified, however, a person cannot suppress the attendant biochemical consequences.

Doctors are studying the biochemical basis of anxiety and anxiety neurosis. The neurotic reacts with fear out of proportion to the situation. In such people, information processed by the cortical and limbic centers appears to activate the G.A.S., inappropriately, leading to increased adrenaline production.

The biochemical changes of the alarm or fight/flight reaction include the release from the body's fat deposits of free fatty acids to be used as fuel for the coming expenditure of energy. Increase in the amount of fats present in the bloodstream contributes to coronary disease. High concentration of fatty acids in the blood is associated with high blood pressure, heart attacks, and strokes. Hypertension, a chronic condition in which psychic stressors apparently play an important role, is the most common of all the circulatory disorders. Today close to 24 million suffer from it, and 700,000 Americans die each year from heart disease.[9]

In a society that is very much stress-oriented, we must learn to develop the means to moderate the negative effects of stress on our physical as well as our psychological well-being. Models of behavior that are admired – including ambition, drive, extreme goal orientation, financial success, aggression and the appearance of being constantly busy – nevertheless contribute to a high level of stress. However, as times passes many people are realizing that this is not the way they want to spend their lives and are looking for other approaches to happiness and fulfillment.

It is for this reason that more and more people are turning toward religion and meditative techniques. Some feel that life does not have to be so complicated. The widespread human-potential and self-exploration movements and a renewed search for spiritual growth seem to indicate that people are looking for new values in life, rather than those designed by modern society, or simply values to help them cope with the pressures of everyday life.

For most people, it is not possible to make a major change in their lives in order to eliminate the sources of stress, since to do so might involve a divorce, a change of job, friends, environment, philosophy, and even goals. Not many people are strong enough or free enough of commitments to others, or willing to give up the security of a place or a job. Therefore, instead of finding solutions, most people turn to alcohol and drugs.

Unfortunately, drugs can be addictive. They may hide stress responses for a limited time, but they do not train one to prevent the situation from arising again. *Drugs make one dependent, not independent.*

For the common disorder of simple nervous tension, an alarming number of tranquilizers and barbiturates are prescribed each year. A recent statistics indicated 144 million new prescriptions are written each year for psychotropic drugs, including anti-depressants, minor and major tranquilizers. Millions of Americans are virtually on drug maintenance for alleviation of nervous tension, and spend a great part of their waking activity in a sedative state.[10]

In spite of their vast use, these drugs do not seem to provide a cure. In a seminar on Psychology, Psychotherapy, and Sufism in 1987 in Los Angeles, Dr. Lynn Wilcox, a psychologist and professor at California State University, Sacramento, said,

Research has not been able to substantiate the claims of psychotherapeutic helpfulness. The so-called 'cure' rate is not impressive. Temporary changes are sometimes seen, but permanent change is elusive. Therefore, some people go from therapist to therapist, from workshop to workshop, from seminar to seminar. It seems analogous to eating a good meal. The stomach is temporarily filled, but hunger soon recurs.

Psychologists merely treat the symptoms of the disease, from behavior problems to deep depressions and abnormalities of character. A medical superintendent of a sanatorium says, "We specialists are too wrapped up in our technical work. What we need is a doctor alongside us to treat the souls of our patients.[11]" Yet wouldn't it be better if every doctor, however specialized, treated the whole "person" of his patient? Wouldn't it be better to treat the patient rather than the disease? Not just to relieve the symptoms temporarily but to find the roots and the causes of the disease? A related question is: What qualifications must such a doctor possess? And since "psyche" means "soul," are the academic qualifications of psychologist sufficient to treat the soul of a person?

"Psychology is today commonly defined as a branch of science that attempts to study human behavior, acts, or mental processes," says Dr. Lynn Wilcox, a Psychologist and Professor at California State University, Sacramento.

This is an extremely broad area of study, including all the complexities of human existence, from the reflex actions of a newborn to the motivations for declaring war.

Unable to determine any basic underlying principles governing human behavior, psychologists have more or less divided up the area, each specializing in the study of one small segment of human behavior. Physiological psychologists study the structure of the human eye, just as some physicians do. Perceptual psychologists study how our eyes deceive us in perception. Industrial psychologists attempt to determine how to increase work productivity. Educational psychologists try and measure what they call intelligence, and so forth. The goal of all psychology, expressed in every beginning psychology text, is prediction and control of human behavior. The academic area of psychology devotes itself to attempting to predict and control human behavior. In so doing, it studies only what is quantifiable, that is, that which can in some way be physically measured.

Psychology essentially studies the physiological functioning of the central nervous system, including the brain. Although psychologists have provided useful information on psychological functioning and useful descriptions of human behavior in various circumstances, psychological experts disagree in their opinions about every question of importance, such as: 'What is mental illness?' 'What is creativity?' 'What is intelligence?' This is one reason why what is called 'psychology' frequently changes. The second reason is that psychology is based on theory, that is, on some individual person's ideas about human behavior, from which he or she constructs a model they believe to be correct. As ideas change, so does the theory.

There are today several hundred approaches to choose from: psychoanalytic, Gestalt, client-centered, behavioral, rational-emotive, neurolinguistic programming, existential, to name just a few,[12] concludes Dr. Lynn Wilcox.

In a meeting of medical superintendents of sanatoriums, specialists who have obtained good results with a treatment noted that they were disappointed to see patients leave the sanatorium and take up their normal lives again, only to be back a few months later. Several doctors at the meeting therefore suggested that the patients should be kept in the

> sanatorium for longer periods. But it is obvious that a patient whose physical illness has been cleared cannot be withheld indefinitely from return to normal life. However, it too often happens that the patient's 'home' leads to a relapsed, caused by returning to his family and his social environment where all the problems whose solutions he had been unable to find before still exist.[13]

Therefore an individual needs to be examined physically, mentally, and spiritually in order that as much understanding as possible about his relationship with his total environment can be discovered. This environment includes his family, peers, job situation, living situation, his concept of himself and his role in society, and his goals. The causes of distress have to be determined. Many times, the stresses that affect us overlap and intertwine, making it difficult to determine their sources. It is not enough for a psychologist to merely listen to a patient. It is the cause of distress that has to be identified. It is not sufficient for a physician to relieve psychosomatic disease by drugs; again, the source has to be determined.

> Modern medicine has tended to view man as a machine with interchangeable parts, and has developed sophisticated procedures for repairing, removing, or artificially constructing these parts. These are significant achievements, but in the process the healing professions have lost sight of man as a dynamic, integrated, and complex system with marked capacity for self-healing.[14]

Consideration of the whole person emphasizes the healing process, the maintenance of health, and the prevention of illness. An ancient concept in Eastern culture, this idea of preventive health care is one that is beginning to emerge in the West where it is considered as one of the most important innovations in medical research and its clinical application.

Results of the research on self-healing have changed the way many people view treatment and recovery. "The more I look, the more I'm convinced that emotions are running the show. Cancer strikes people who give up hope when faced with stress," Candace Pert told patients at his Cancer Counseling and Research Center in Dallas. "If you want to recover, you must learn to be tenacious in fighting your disease and hopeful about the outcome. That means undergoing counseling to learn to deal with social and emotional problems. It means setting goals and finding reasons to live.

Stress can make a person sick, depressed people are more likely to get cancer, and positive thinking promotes survival."

"I think about 'life' not death, "answers one of the AIDS patients of the Sufi Master Hazrat Salaheddin Ali Nader Angha when a friend asked why he had started school again with such a terminal condition.

Psychoneuro-immunology [PNI] researchers investigate how the brain effects the body's immune cells. Drawing on the most sophisticated techniques of psychology, neurobiology, and immunology, these researchers have shown that the brain can send signals along nerves to enhance defenses against infection and pump out chemicals that make the body more aggressive against disease. And since these pathways can be turned on and off by thoughts and emotions, they say, it's no surprise that mental states can alter the course of an illness.

PNI studies have demonstrated that the brain and the immune system make up a closed circuit. Not only can the brain's chemicals regulate immune defenses, but communication can also go the other way, from the immune system to the brain. In this manner the immune system can act as a sensory organ, sending chemical messages about bacteria, viruses, and tumors all over the body. During an infection, the researchers believe, immune cells not only fight invading organisms but also affect brain-controlled functions like heart rate, sleep, and body temperature. Signals from the immune system may even reach the emotional and rational centers of the brain, explaining perhaps the cause of irritability, and why mental capacity deteriorates at the same time as resistance to infection. The brain controls the immune system the same way that it controls behavioral activities, concludes immunologist Gerard Renoux of the University of Tours, France.

Obviously, no one would deny that having to cope with a serious disease affects a patient psychologically. But the connections between the brain and the immune system suggest that something physiological is going on as well. Since the brain can talk to immune cells, a patient's state of mind can, in a concrete way, determine the status of immunological defenses.[15]

In light of these findings, more physicians are now acknowledging the connection between mind and body. "Feelings are chemical," says Dr. Bernie Siegel, the author of *Love, Medicine and Miracles* and a surgeon. "Feeling good about life helps us physically." Statements like these from physicians would have been surprising even just a few years ago. But with the many new research findings and case studies being documented in medical journals, the practice of self-healing is now receiving much more serious attention from the doctors than before. With the concept of self-healing now becoming more accepted within the medical community and physicians realizing the importance of the mind in the healing process, many open-minded physicians are working with their patients in finding ways to fully utilize this new method of treatment.

Studies have shown that 75 percent of all doctor visits are due to stress-related symptoms, and the worst kind of chronic stress is helplessness. Self-healing techniques often provide the individual with an increased sense of control over his or her illness, which reduces feelings of helplessness.

Once an individual understands that he is an active and responsible participant in the process of self-healing, he is no longer the passive victim of a disease or the passive recipient of a cure. The patient has to be guided and shown that he is responsible for his own health, lifestyle, and future, in which he can become an active participant through meditation and self-healing and by gaining awareness of who he is and what he needs. Carl Jung says, "The horizons of the human psyche embraces infinitely more than a limited purview of the doctor's consulting room. The cure ought to grow naturally out of each person and patient himself."[16]

Medicine is legally defined in terms of the diagnosis and treatment of disease. This is but one aspect of health. An individual must assume responsibility for his mental and physical well-being. According to the ancient Chinese philosopher Lao-tse, "The journey of a thousand miles begins with one step," and that initial acceptance of responsibility and commitment to oneself is a prerequisite for individual growth and transformation.

The ancient mystics, or Sufis, believed that man has inherited total knowledge of existence, but that to claim his inheritance and birthright, he must grow and develop consciously. He has inner potential and abilities that enable him to shape his environment. He is capable of gaining the knowledge of self-awareness. This is different from the premise of most traditional kinds of therapy, in which the attitude is that the patient is "sick," the therapist is the all-knowing "authority," and he cures the patient by outside help and support. In contrast to this, the Eminent Hazrat Ali, whose guidance we follow in the School of Sufism, states that, "Each individual has his or her own truth, and cure within oneself." And Buddha says "Find prosperity within." Therefore, man's will helps him reach higher realms of life. The path to tranquility and happiness lies within each of us. Any type of help acquired from outside, even the best and the least harmful, is but temporary. For a wound must begin to heal from within. Then, medications are applied in order to avoid infection, but the renewal of the tissues is a healing process that takes place from within. Similarly, the body's excellent immune system fights viruses even before the rise of temperature in the body makes us aware of any abnormalities. In the same way, we are able to fight mental pressures using the body's energy fields. These energy fields play an important role in our physical, mental, and psychic well-being. This will be explained in Chapter Eight.

CHAPTER SEVEN ENDNOTES

1.   Shah Maghsoud Sadegh Angha, *Psalm of Gods*, from the collection of *The Mystery of Humanity*, University Press of America, Inc., 1986, p. 53.

2.   C. William Chittick, *The Sufi Path of Love: The Spiritual Teachings of Rumi*, State University of New York Press, Albany, 1983, p. 339.

3.   Chittick, p. 348.

4.   Frederick Nietzsche, *Thus Spoke Zarathustra*, Penguin Books Limited, NY, 1982, p. 66.

5.   Shah Maghsoud Sadegh Angha, *Psalm of Gods*, p. 53.

6.   Salaheddin Ali Nader Angha , *Peace*, introduction.

7.   Jackie Swartz, *Letting go of Stress*, Pinnacle Books, Inc., New York, NY, 10018, 1982, p. 9.

8.   Harold H. Bloomfield, et al., *TM Discovering Inner Energy and Overcoming Stress*, Delacorte Press, New York, New York, 1975, p. 51.

9.   *Ibid.*, pp. 50-53.

10.   Kenneth R. Pelletier, p. 20.   "Mind as Healer, Mind as Slayer," Dell publishing, 1977.

11.   Paul Tournier, Edwin Hudson, trans., *The Healing of Persons*, Harper & Row Publishers, Inc., New York, New York, p. 21.

12.   Lynn Wilcox, seminar, "Psychology, Psychotheraphy & Sufism", LA, 1987.

13.   Paul Tournier, Edwin Hudson, trans., *The Healing of Persons*, Harper & Row Publishers, Inc., New York, New York, p. 21.

14.   Pelletier, p. 12.

15.   Rob Wechsler, "A New Prescription: Mind over Malady," *Discover*, Feb. 1987, pp. 51-58.

16.   C. Carl Jung, *Thoughts, Reflections, Dreams*.

CHAPTER EIGHT

HEALTH: A BALANCED ENERGY FLOW IN THE BODY

*The basic law of life is motion, the rhythmic,
cyclic pulsation of radiant energy, which is the
basic building block of our bodies.*

Jack Schwartz

To understand how to win the war against stress and fight off opposing forces from within, it is necessary to learn about "human energy fields," and "auric fields." Then we will understand how the last stage of Hans Selye's G.A.S., the expenditure of energy and the stage of exhaustion, can be avoided. The process of self-healing will be introduced in this chapter.

Jack Schwartz explains,

With progress in modern science, we are becoming more and more aware that the human organism is not just a physical structure made up of molecules, that we are electromagnetic and electrochemical beings made up of energy fields. Our bodies may appear to be solid and opaque, but if we could magnify the cells, molecules, and atoms of which we are composed, we would see that at the most fundamental level we are made up of energy, of electrochemical and electromagnetic activity that is constantly going on in our bodies.

If electricity is the force behind our electromagnetic energy fields, then magnetism is the direction-giving aspect of that force. There is increasing scientific evidence for this view of human energy fields. For years, scientists have been able to detect the energy emitted by the body by measuring skin potentials. In order to measure the electrical output of various organs, researchers place electrodes on the skin. To measure the electrical output of the brain, for example, electrodes are placed on the forehead and the scalp in the cerebral area.

Similarly, the electrocardiogram measures the electrical output of the heart through electrodes placed on the skin of the chest wall; the polygraph, or lie detector, measures the changes in the electrical potential of the skin, or the galvanic skin resistance. In all these cases, we are not sure exactly what is being measured but we do know that we are measuring a form of radiation; we would not be able to measure it if it were not radiant, or electromagnetic, energy. But because all these measurements are taken using skin potentials, we are not really accurately measuring the output of the organism itself; we get interference from the skin that lies between our instruments and the organ whose output is being measured.

We now have a better method of measuring the electromagnetic output of the body. Instead of using skin potentials, the electromagnetic forces around the body are measured directly. This is done with highly sensitive instruments. This is done in a unit of magnetism known as the *gauss*. Of course, earth itself radiates electromagnetic energy. Every particle on earth, even though it may appear solid and stationary to us, has continual activity taking place within it; it looks solid and dense because the energy is of high frequency and low amplitude.

Besides the energy outputs that have been measured outside the body, there are other subtle forces acting within the body that are not yet understood by science. The Soviet researcher, Dr. Alexander Dubrov, has found that during mitosis, or the splitting of cells, there is photon radiation from the cells. Photons are particle waves of light. The radiation produces a dim glow. The photon emissions produced by the cells in our bodies are the ultraviolet frequencies, beyond what we know as the visible spectrum. All the trillions of cells in our bodies are emitting such photons, from one to another.[1]

"There are two main factors that have direct influence upon cellular life," says Hazrat Shah Maghsoud Sadegh Angha, a teacher of the Oveyssi School of Sufism, which was founded 1,400 years ago.

These are nutrition and temperature, serving as the experimental basis for all research and present investigations concerning life. However, we cannot overlook the influences of cosmic and ultracosmic rays, the planets, and finally, all the universal gravities acting upon the cellular cycle.

Can the condensed powers in one atom of hydrogen be conceived or measured? The condensed powers in one atom of hydrogen are acquired from the sun or cosmic and ultracosmic radiations in an initial atom. Since, in my opinion, the reality of life has to be shown in the hydrogen atom or in its compositions, and cell organizations are formed of four kinds of hydrogen compositions, these condensed powers (which are in direct contact from within the cell to external energies), prove to be an agent of life on the earth. Therefore, discovery of the cell life is impossible without recognizing these powers and their influences.

Other factors directly influencing cell life are the magnetic sources of the human body. Numbering thirteen, these main sources are in direct connection with all universal magnetic and electric fields.[2]

For more clarification, let us consider the following example. Just as power stations distribute current through extended wire cables, magnetic sources play their part in the human body as substations. They transform the acquired energies into magnetism and other essential conditions of the body. The tender materials of the body, such as magnetic substances, act both as transmitters and receivers; each is either effected or effective. Therefore, if any disorder in these magnetic sources should appear, the body's magnetics and its nervous system would not be able to perform their communicative functions properly, and the body would become defective.

Health depends on energy flow. For energy to be transformed from one state to another, it must flow constantly through the body. As mentioned above, the magnetic sources of the body provide the impetus for this flow. When these centers stagnate or when their function is impeded, the body's aura of energy, its radiant output, is distorted. An analogy is what happens to stagnant water where there is no flow and movement. The basic law of life is motion, the rhythmic, cyclic pulsation of radiant energy, which is the basic building block of our bodies as it is of the universe. Illness can be characterized as a stagnation of this energy, when energy is not being heightened and transformed.

The body ingests nourishment in a heavy form because the body is heavy. A more subtle body assimilates finer energy. But the human body has the potential and the task of transforming the energy it digests into more subtle energy. We are not bound to the heaviness of our organism, for we have the capacity to transform the energy within ourselves into finer and finer levels. We have abused our natural birthright if we cut ourselves off from the finer nourishments, or energy, surrounding us.

Our bodies are composed of, for the most part, water. The processes of this mass of water, which flows through our body, are of the utmost importance because the body fluids act as a catalyst, carrying and adjusting all external influences and nutrition throughout every part of the body. Furthermore, the paramagnetic quality of our body fluids depends on a constant process of the creation and combination of ions in this fluid and the maintenance of the ionic balance.

To make changes in the body, then, means to change the electromagnetic state of the body's fluid. Electricity is the particular characteristic of the energy force we are dealing with, and magnetism is the direction given to that force. Disease, old age, and other alterations in the body's energy pattern are ultimately traceable to imbalances and declines in the electrical potency of the body plasma, its intermolecular fluid.[3]

The condition of health is thus a regulated, balanced flow of energy through the body, which receives its impetus from the energy centers. Moreover, there is radiant energy emitted by the body, and this radiant electromagnetic energy bears a specific relation to the location and intensity of the activity within the body. When we realize that our bodies are in fact made up of nothing but energy in constant transformation, it is easier to understand how subtle, non-physical, energetic influences such as emotions and thoughts can have an effect on our emotional and mental experiences. Similarly, once we understand what produces the radiant emanation from our bodies, it is clearer why this emanation should reveal something about the state of our functioning. People with no particular psychic gifts can learn to see the ray and the aura around the body. This information can be of tremendous help to counselors or to those who treat physical illness because the subtle energy fields that surround the human body can convey advance warning of problems that may not yet have manifested themselves physically and in any case understanding of the energy fields can aid in a clearer perception of what is really amiss in a case of mental, emotional, or physical illness.[4]

Health, therefore, is not just the absence of disease, it is a dynamic, evolutionary process, a state of constant change. You are made up of some 350 trillion cells, each unique and each with capacity to maintain and reproduce itself and to interact and interrelate with all the other cells of the body. Every particle that makes up the components of the cell is in a state of constant activity, and there is a constant flow of energy arising from that activity. Because health is equivalent to the free, unimpeded flow of energy, you can see that it is possible to interfere with your health, to make yourself ill by intervening on the subtlest, least-material level.[5]

The Swedish radiologist Nordenstrom posits what seems an astounding theory:

The human body contains the equivalent of electric circuits. As Nordenstrom describes his body electric, the circuits are switched on by an injury, an infection, or a tumor, or even by the normal activity of the body's organs; voltages build and fluctuate; electric currents course through the arteries and veins and across capillary walls, drawing white blood cells and metabolic compounds into and out of surrounding tissues. This electrical system, says Nordenstrom, works to balance the activity of the internal organs and, in the case of injuries, represents the very foundation of the healing process. In his view, it's as critical to the well-being of the human body as the flow of blood. Disturbances in this electrical network, he suggests, may be involved in the development of cancer and other diseases.

Classical medicine certainly doesn't deny that there are myriad electrical forces at work within the body, in addition to chemical ones exerted by hormones and enzymes, and physical ones like the pressure of the blood in the arteries and veins. Every human thought and action is accompanied by the conduction of the electrical signals along the fibers of the nervous system. Indeed, life wouldn't exist without the constant flow of ions across the membranes of cells. Yet Nordenstrom argues that the picture is incomplete. As he sees it, medical research has provided a descriptive view of the chemical and physical processes at work in the human body, but hasn't explained how they're interrelated. It is a picture of effects without causes. In Nordenstrom's view, the cause behind many of the effects is the ebb and flow in his biologically closed electric circuits.

If he is right, these circuits may explain many fundamental regulatory processes in the human body, and even the seemingly inexplicable therapeutic effects of acupuncture and of electromagnetic fields.

To prove that his theory is more than just an academic curiosity, Nordenstrom has put his ideas to work, using electricity to treat lung and breast tumors. Considering the immaturity of his science, he has had remarkable success. He is also developing techniques for combining electrical treatment with chemotherapy, using the electrodes to concentrate the chemical around the tumor.[6]

We can therefore claim that although, at first glance, human beings seem to possess only a physical body, science as well as religion tells us this is not the whole picture. In fact, the physical body is the most superficial dimension of man's being. The body needs to receive a balanced diet in order to maintain its equilibrium, but nutrition alone is not enough. An overall balance has to be achieved to ensure the best possible health since the human body consists of different auras that surround the physical body. Each of these auric bodies is nurtured through the flow of energy from invisible energy centers mentioned before. A healthy and balanced energy flow throughout the body assures a radiant auric body.

CHAPTER EIGHT ENDNOTES

1.   Jack Schwarz, *Human Energy Systems*, E. P. Dutton, New York, New York, 1980, pp. 1-3.

2.   Shah Maghsoud Angha, *The Hidden Angles of Life*, Multidisciplinary Publications, Pomona, Calif., pp. 56-58.

3.   Schwarz, pp. 89 and 91.

4.   *Ibid.*, p. 21.

5.   *Ibid.*, p. 108.

6.   Gary Taubes, *An Electrifying Possibility, Discover*, April 1986, p. 22.

CHAPTER NINE

THE ENERGY CENTERS IN THE BODY

The most important energy source in the body is the heart, the "source of life."

Hazrat Shah Maghsoud Sadegh Angha

In this chapter we will discuss in detail the function of the energy centers and the different bodies surrounding the physical mold: the auric fields. As a result we will discover how to fight stress and to prevent the last stage of Hans Selye's "exhaustion" by means of activating the energy centers existent in the body and the conservation of that energy to gain inner balance. However, in this chapter and in the next, the theoretical explanation of these energy centers is given; its practice will be introduced later.

"The health of the organs and regular functions of the cells must be secured by providing a suitable equilibrium in the magnetic functions and assimilation and repulsion of the body,"[1] according to Hazrat Shah Maghsoud Sadegh Angha in *The Hidden Angles of Life*.

The tasks of the body's energy centers are:

1)   absorbing and storing the subtle electromagnetic energies from the surrounding energy fields (i.e., solar, cosmic or ultracosmic);

2)   breaking down and transforming those energies into a form that can be used by the body; and

3)   distribution of the transformed energy throughout the body to nourish each cell.

The cells, in turn, use that transformed energy to balance their activities.

The law governing this energy exchange is one of conservation and balance of input and output. A malfunction in this system, caused either by a low input of energy, a dysfunction in energy transformation, or an uneven distribution, will cause disorder at the cellular level. In such a case the body's magnetic and nervous systems are immediately deficient.

When an energy center is operating in a balanced manner, the color of the aura surrounding it will be very pale and pure. If a center is not properly transmitting energy, the color will have a dense, dark outflow, apparent in the aura.

For an optimal utilization of energy, all the energy centers should be functioning in a balanced, fully operative manner. Our energy centers are never completely blocked or closed. If no energy at all could flow through, we would die. If one of these energy centers slows down, the energy flow will be impeded and organs will begin to show signs of illness. The energy centers' interaction with the endocrine glands maintains the normal function of the body's organs. Because the unimpeded energy flow through the energy centers is the key to optimal health, we must realize that the attitudes, fears and anxieties that impede the flow can be just as damaging as actual physical injury to an organ.

Let us at this time take a closer look at these energy centers and try to understand their function individually and as a whole. This we will do according to the instructions given in *The Hidden Angles of Life*, which is written by the Sufi Master, Hazrat Shah Maghsoud Sadegh Angha.

ENERGY CENTERS

Thirteen main energy centers connect human beings with universal magnetic and electric fields, through which the body is constantly in contact with the currents of existence. The Sufi discipline considers the following centers to be the most important.

Solar Plexus

The *solar plexus* is in the pit under the sternum and over the diaphragm. The diaphragm serves as a sort of boundary between man's lower, more "instinctive" nature and his higher centers, which become increasingly related in a more evolved consciousness. The diaphragm separates the subtle from the dense; it literally separates the sensitive organs, such as the heart and lungs, from the digestive and purgative organs. The lower part of this borderline has been defined in the Koran as the "earth," the upper part, the "heaven." If we define the earth as the plane in which the laws of physics, action, and reaction govern, then heaven represents infinity and the most subtle state of existence. The same as ice, water, and vapor are one in essence but when their molecules are packed closely together, it becomes dense and takes the shape of ice; the more the molecules expand it becomes more and more subtle, almost invisible as vapor.

This important energy center, the solar plexus, that is located on the boundary of the heaven and the earth, is nourished by the heart, and it nourishes the liver and the organs.

The "solar plexus" is so named because it is associated with fire. "Solar" refers to the sun, its means of nourishment. The solar plexus is a sort of internal sun produced by the oxidation or "burning" of food. Plants take their energy directly from the sun, but human beings and animals must produce their own energy. When human beings eat they take the energy trapped in plant matter and release it through the chemical process of digestion. This creates an "inner flame," which provides the energy for maintaining life. When this inner flame is properly regulated, it allows the person to be healthy, to digest his food properly, and to have a consistent energy level without being easily fatigued.

This center primarily serves as a receptor of the principle force of vitality that enters the physical body. Its magnetic particles are directly fostered by sunlight. Because the activities of the solar plexus, as well as all other energy centers, are directly related to the nerve tracts, all cells, globules and finally the entire organism depend completely on receiving the magnetic waves of the sun. Thus by the help of solar energy many diseases can be treated.

Focusing one's thoughts on the solar plexus increases the concentration of the energy there. The concentration of energy speeds up the action of the digestive organs and improves their ability to secrete enzymes and process food.

Poor digestion may mean an inadequate focus of energy in the area of the solar plexus. Energy is ordinarily stored at this solar plexus center. When the solar plexus center is energized, one feels dynamic and assertive.

The Center at the Base of the Spine

Another magnetic source is at the last vertebra of the spinal column. Some thinkers seem to believe that this triangular cartilage is an effective agent for the being of mankind and is one of the important centers of life and has a structure which will not be transformed to soil after death.

In any case, the vital organization of its cells possesses a complicated composition. This magnetic source is the center for exertion of powers, and it is impressive in genesis and reproduction.

> In previous beliefs and religions, and even in Islam, extra importance has been given to this triangular magnetic source. The yogi, for example, concentrates on his spinal column, which is very effective. However, in Sufism the process of concentration will be performed on the source of life, in the heart, and the magnetic source of the solar plexus, and then will be expanded to the brain. This kind of unification and method belongs exclusively to the 'Oveyssi School of Sufism,' and this method resembles the instructions given by the prophets.[2]

The Source between the Eyebrows

The third of these energy centers is located at the pit between the eyebrows, which is directly in contact with the cartilages of the nose. Concentration and gathering of magnetics in this source, produce telepathy, the ability to read the thoughts of others, and is related to the "sixth sense."

Concerning "extrsensory" perception, Hazrat Shah Maghsoud says that cognition is the ability to conceive of magnetic rays or waves that come to us from our surroundings. These waves pass through all materials and objects without the need of a natural substance. He also says a "clairvoyant" is one who has control over a part of his brain and can conceive the rays from a certain point. This is like a wireless receptor. Of all the existing waves, he will receive the appointed and desired wave.

This is in reference to the coordination between physical and spiritual ability, as a result of which the brain becomes susceptible to receive any special magnetic waves. Obviously essential fundamentals and conditions are necessary for both the sender and the receiver systems. For example, if some tremblings of sound are broadcast on a special wavelength, a receiver will get the waves on a channel, but these sound waves are of no use to an insensitive or deaf ear, although these broadcast waves are distributed throughout space and surround the earth's atmosphere. This example is comparable to any scientific transaction and activity. Our orbit is full of metaphysical and physical events, but our knowledge about them is small. Our physical and mental system of knowledge is far too ill-equipped to understand the way things happen, or are inspired and discovered.

> Eastern, clear-sighted, and intuitive scientists believe that if all of man's natural powers and strengths were concentrated on a precise metaphysical point of existence or became accustomed to comprehending truth superior to sensual limitations and animal habits he would be able to discover more clearly and precisely those natural principles that have metaphysical terms, because naturally the sum total of strength is much more powerful than scattered energy.
>
> When man reaches this level of concentration, or, when the power of organized existence comes under the will of the intellect or the rational mind, then he will be able to comprehend and discover energies beyond even waves, and he will be able to comprehend the spirit and divinity of himself and all in the depth of his mind and soul. All that is hidden from him now shall manifest to him.[3]

Let us go on to the next important energy center at the top of the head.

The Source in the Upper Fontanel

This magnetic source at the top of the head acts as a radar, and consequently it can contact the spreading waves of thoughts in space. According to Hazrat Shah Maghsoud, discoveries and inventions occur by concentration of this source and its connection to the magnetic source located between the eyebrows.

This magnetic source may transmit the magnetic waves of the brain up to 12 kilometers or more in space in the form of a luminous column. Alpha waves, after contacting this magnetic source and communicating with sub-sources, cause hearing, smelling and seeing waves that are invisible to the limited senses and other supernatural events. A connection of the cerebral cortex and the bounded solar system to the diameter of three billion kilometers is certain, and it is in constant contact with the alpha and other mental waves that are called the *bounded area of illuminated thought* by Hazrat Shah Maghsoud Sadegh Angha in *The Hidden Angles of Life*.

> The custom of placing an ornate crown on the head of a monarch seems to be rooted in the idea that the person with an evolved consciousness should be the one to lead the state. This is the concept of the 'philosopher king.' A reverence for this center of consciousness is also seen in the symbology of certain religions. In the Christian tradition, it has been customary for certain monks to shave the crown of the head and leave a bare circle. In the Jewish tradition, a skull cap is worn that covers that same area. Religious art often highlights the area of the crown with a burst of light or a halo. The Hopi Indians say of man's relationship to this center:

>> 'Here, when he was born, was the soft spot, the "open door," through which he received his life and communicated with his Creator. At the time of the last phase of his creation, the soft spot was hardened and the door was closed. The yogi tradition gives a similar significance to the soft spot of the infant, noting that it gradually hardens as the child's intuitive qualities are diminished during the development of rationality and ego functions. The yogic viewpoint, however, emphasizes that this door may be reopened.'[4]

The Source At The Head of the Medulla Oblongata

This magnetic source is situated at the head of the medulla oblongata, the first vertebra of the cervical spine in the neck. This energy center connects directly with the energy source, that is in the last vertebra in the spinal column. The harmonization and the communication of these two pivots result in extraordinary actions practiced in India. Some samples that indicate extraordinary power are the yogi who rests on a bed of nails and survives on one date a day; another by he who holds out his hand to stop a train that is moving.

The Source of Life

The most important energy source in the body is the *heart*. Hazrat Shah Maghsoud Sadegh Angha calls it the "source of life." The heart is known as a wise and powerful manager, containing intelligence, and, most important of all, is connected to all magnetic sources.

This magnetic source is the celestial center in man. Most religions place "Heaven in the human heart." Molavi, the famous Sufi poet, says:

O pilgrims where are thee, where are thee?
Ka'ba is here, here you should be, here you should be.

Ka'ba is the house of God that pilgrims visit in Mecca. However, a Sufi believes that it is not enough to visit the house alone, but that one must also visit God, the owner of the house. When the Sufi poet says *Ka'ba is here* he is indicating that God dwells in the heart of each of us, that we do not have to travel a distance but need only travel in the land of our hearts to find and meet him. Revelations only take place in the heart, without the interference of the senses. God confirms this in the Koran,

All Heaven and Earth may not be vast enough to bear
His divine Presence but the heart of the righteous man will.
The Koran also says,

Have they not traveled in the land
so that they should have hearts,
with which to understand,
Or ears with which to hear?
For surely, it is not the eyes that are blind,
But blind are the hearts,
which are in the breasts.
(Koran surah 22:46)

The Bible says,

Do you not know that you are God's temple
And that God dwells in you?
(Corinthians 3:16)

And the Koran says,

Or say: He has forged a lie against Allah?
So if Allah please,

He would seal thy heart.
And Allah blots out the falsehood,
And confirms,
the Truth with His words,
Surely He is Knower,
Of what is in the breasts.
(Koran surah 42:24)

Whey My servants ask thee concerning Me,
I am indeed close:
I listen to the prayer of every suppliant,
When he calleth on Me:
Let them also, with a will,
Listen to My call.
(Koran surah 2:186)

Say: Whoever is an enemy to Gabriel,
For he brings down
The revelation to thy heart
By God's will,
A conformation of what went before,
And guidance and glad tidings
For those who believe.
(Koran surah 2:97)

Thenceforth were your hearts hardened
They became like a rock,
And even worse in hardness.
For among rocks,
There are some from which,
Rivers gush forth,
Others, there are when split,
Asunder send forth water,
And others which sink,
For fear of God,
And God is not unmindful of what ye do.
(Koran surah 2:74)

Hazrat Shah Maghsoud Sadegh Angha explains that

love is a penetrating, electric, or magnetic power that joins all
the particles of the infinite together. In fact all existence is
originated by the power of love. Without the existence of this
force of attraction, it would be absolutely true to say not a
single particle could come into existence. Love is the basic
characteristic of every manifestation. Love exists in three
stages. The origin of love and desires on the materialistic level
is the magnetic source of the 'solar plexus.' A more superior
kind of love occurs with the complete unification of the two
magnetic sources of the brain, and the solar plexus. Love is a
description of life in its most subtle state. This superior form

of love is called 'spiritual love.' The spiritual love results in the unification of the two magnetic sources of the brain, the heart, and the solar plexus and their unified effects on all the magnetic and nervous systems in an extensive cooperation. Disorder and a lack of harmony occur, however, when each of these sources performs separate functions. One's eternal identity is discovered when unification and equilibrium are established between the outward and inward, the individual and universal powers. Then, it is assured that many of the spiritual matters will be discovered through laboratory experiments on both the magnetic centers and sources of the atom, as well as the universe. At this time, the gates of the unknown world will open wide. 'If the research of the spiritualists had been started from this point, many biological problems would have been solved long before now.'[5]

Therefore, health should be achieved through the balance of personal magnetics instead of customarily following an ambiguous psychological philosophy by establishing a link between experiences gained from this ambiguity and physiological medicine. This is the right path that the medical sciences should pursue.

At the present time, the Sufi Master of the School of Oveyssi is busy with spiritual healing, transmitting magnetic energies to patients, and thus strengthening them. In Chapter Eleven we will talk about the healing processes the Sufi Master Hazrat Salaheddin Nader Angha is using on the AIDS patients he is treating.

> Concentration of the vital energies of man on any of the mentioned energy sources has its own extraordinary effects, and generally similar effects are found less in inferior animals in comparison to the human being. The dispersion of the magnetic energies makes human beings appear weaker than even animals, while it is not so. For example, animals are aware, in some circumstances, one or two hours before an earthquake. This is because of their senses and animal nature, but perfect men are aware of many events before their happenings by their concentration of internal and external energies.
>
> Discovering future events and keeping past incidents in sight depends on being an observer in the present. In Sufism this is called breaking the limited boundaries through the infinite. In other words, when a human being succeeded in overcoming the speed of light he would gain knowledge about all life manifestations past and future.
>
> For example, when I was in the presence of my great teacher, my father, Hazrat Mir Ghotbeddin Mohammad Angha, in 1961, he uttered:

'I am hearing the sound of cries and mourns and see many people being buried alive under ruins.'

Exactly a week later, a destructive and horrible earthquake hit, which shook a large area about 1,000 kilometers sixty kilometers from Teheran. The earthquake ruined the area and killed nearly 10,000 people.

Just as different organs of the body are interrelated and effect each other, and each have their individual function, these sources are also interrelated and effective in the same manner. Therefore, the fields of their effects are perpetual from the body to the magnetic particles and vice versa. The first stage of the physiological death of the body can also be rendered by the disconnection of these energy transmitters of the body.

It should not be imagined that the human being is only a material organization. However, the magnetic connection of the body has been considered man's spiritual connections by some researchers while the independent identity of man, the soul, that governs the body and is the active and wise force that manifests through each person has been overlooked.[6]

Therefore, Hazrat Shah Maghsoud proposes, "In order to discover life and its mysteries, the material laboratory experiences should be used as an introduction, and the book of creation should be studied from the first chapters to discover the repelling and receiving of human magnetic, cosmic energies by the particles, and how they assist the extensive equilibrium of life."[7]

CHAPTER NINE ENDNOTES

1.   Shah Maghsoud Sadegh Angha, *The Hidden Angles of Life*, p. 62.

2.   *Ibid.*, p. 63.

3.   Shah Maghsoud Sadegh Angha, *The Manifestations of Thought*, pp. 13-14.

4.   Ajaha Swami Rama, *Yoga and Psychotherapy*, pp. 270-271.

5.   Angha, *The Hidden Angles of Life*, pp. 60-62.

6.   Ibid., pp. 70-73.

7.   Ibid., p. 74.

CHAPTER TEN

INNER BALANCE

By activating the existing energy sources to maintain an energy flow in the body and to form strong auras, we form a kind of protective shield around us, that help us fight outside stressors.

The Auric Fields

Man is a complex mechanism composed of physical, etheric, celestial, rational, and luminous bodies. The physical body is only the most superficial dimension of man's being. The higher invisible bodies can help man reach higher spiritual realms.

The etheric body, according to Hazrat Shah Maghsoud, has the shape of the body and is like a mold, formed prior to the formation of the embryo by angels from etheric elements. This is like a thin veil of cloud and floats around the physical body and is rarely detached from it. The etheric body is responsible for innate vitality, transmitting the energies from the sun to the body. It contacts the physical body through the crucial medium of the invisible energy centers mentioned in the previous chapter.

The celestial, rational, and luminous bodies are like three circles inside one another. As the rational soul becomes purer and more gentle, it rises to higher bodies, all of which are in perfect harmony, thus transferring the necessary power and influence for this ascension and goal.

The human aura is thus made up of different levels of density. As we move away from the human body, the energy fields become progressively subtler and more difficult to see. Because of this, we know considerably more about the auras closer to the body than we do about the subtler ones.

We have all had the experience of observing such a multi-leveled energy field. The last time you were looking at a candle flame, for example, you might have noticed different levels of density, represented by varying colors and degrees of subtlety. Light one now and take another look. Right around the wick, a bluish form is surrounded by a dark area that is also bluish-gray. Around that is an oval shape of a golden or yellowish color, and within that yellowish oval, you can see layers of varying degrees of subtlety. Beyond the flame itself, you can see subtle oval-shaped fields of energy as the flame's glow dissipates. The human aura, like the candle flame, is made up of progressively subtle levels of density.

The human body's physical aura may extend as far as 15 or 20 feet, but on the average, the aura is 5 to 8 feet in diameter. In the same way, the marked "halo" that we see around the head of prophets in a religious painting depicts an aura and indicates the connection they have established with the center point of their being, that is, with the source of life within.

Considering once again the tangible image of the candle, we notice how it lights its surroundings and spreads rays. A healthy person has a constant flow of energy and can be said to glow like a candle. The better the energy flow and the less fatigue and stress we feel, the better and healthier we are. A constant energy flow provides the body with ample energy and keeps the body functioning in a state of "inner balance." Therefore, the true solution to stress, lies within each of us. INNER BALANCE is crucial to our health. Just as physical health depends on a balanced diet to maintain its equilibrium, the whole human being needs to establish an emotional and spiritual balance.

An unstable person is like a rickety table. Many techniques of "stress management" are like holding on to the table's legs to keep it from tilting off-balance. The problem is that the table will fall as soon as you let go. Because the table is not secure and cannot stand by itself, it is in constant need of support from an outside source, similar to our fighting stressors by using an outside agent: drugs, alcohol, a vacation, or even the help of a friend. The problem with such agents is they become addictive – even relationships with people – which can frustrate both parties. Addiction is not independence. What we need instead is to acquire stability and independence. Like a study table standing strong on its legs, we need to learn to carry loads without any outside help.

Meditation can give us this balance and strength. By meditating, one gathers all energies within oneself. Meditation results in an even and natural distribution and flow of energy throughout the body and mind, helping to establish stability and balance. By enhancing the auric shield around the body we also prevent it from many physical disorders. This is also a preventive health care measure.

Every atom has   -energy

-electrical charge

-magnetic field

Everything we do scatters the energies

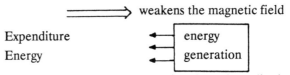

Expenditure   weakens the magnetic field

Energy   energy

generation

Energy generation through meditation

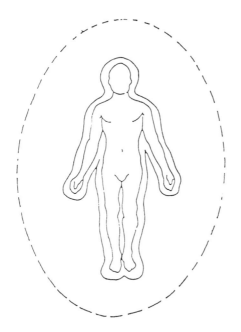

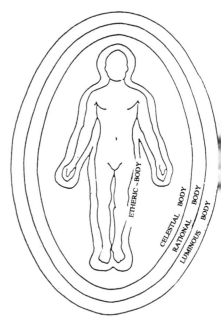

scattered energies   gathered energies
imbalance & weakness   balance & inner strength

The expansion and flow of energy (as shown above) form a shield around the body and act as an immune system to fight stress. By activating our existing energy sources to maintain an energy flow in the body and to form strong auras, we form a kind of protective shield around us.

ILLUSTRATION

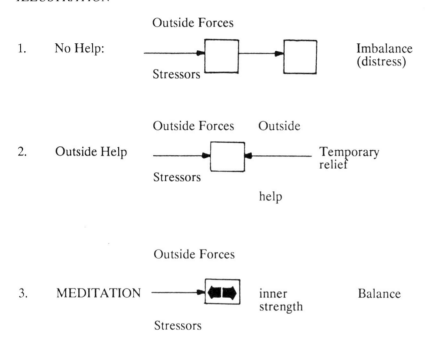

The above diagram represents an individual (the block) under the influence of stress (the stressors.)

1.   An individual under the influence of stress has no outside help in order to cope and withstand the stressors.   The result is distress and imbalance.

2.   The individual still cannot cope with the stressors, but is seeking outside help which presents some temporary relief. This relief is dependent upon the existence of outside help.

3.   Through meditation the individual can stay balanced in the face of the stressors. The inner strength fights the outside stressors, the results of which are balance – calm, serenity.

Meditation

Through balance and equilibrium, we set our mechanism to work effectively enough to activate energy. Through this constant input and output of energy, the auric field is shaped, thus nourishing us as a whole, the body and the soul. If our energy centers do not function well, we cannot generate or emanate energy effectively, as with batteries that are charged only once. After a while, the energy dissipates and the batteries go dead, unless they are activated again. For humans, the recharging process is very important, because our physical, mental, and spiritual health depends upon this constant flow of energy. In his book *The Message from the Soul*, Hazrat Shah Maghsoud says:

> No farmer will block the wells or the springs
> of his farm,
> For if he does, there will be no harvest.[1]

The most important of all the energy centers in the body is the heart, the source of life. "The Kingdom of God is within," said the great prophets. The Kingdom of God is "Heaven" and lives not in images, churches, or books but within us. When all the magnetic energy fields in the body function together as a whole and harmonize with the main source, the heart, an overall health is achieved. And only at this point is one able to realize the "Kingdom of God within," which is complete self-awareness. At this time man is no longer a victim of events and stress he cannot endure but is a pillar of force and serenity. All of which he draws from the spring of life within.

CHAPTER TEN ENDNOTES

1.   Shah Maghsoud Sadegh Angha, *Psalm of Gods*, University Press of America, Inc., Lanham, MD, 1986, p. 44.

CHAPTER ELEVEN

THE ART OF SUFI HEALING AS APPLIED TO "AIDS"

*In the land of our heart the plant
of despair shall never grow.*

Hazrat Salaheddin Ali Nader Angha

In a recent TV interview, Hazrat Salaheddin Ali Nader Angha was asked what he teaches people with AIDS. He responded: "I teach them how to live, not how to die."

Linda O'Riordan, who has been a nurse for 25 years, is involved with the Sacramento AIDS foundation, and is working closely with AIDS patients under the direction of the Spiritual Master of the School of Islamic Sufism, says:

> Concepts, fears, beliefs, and opinions attached to the HIV virus form limits and boundaries. With AIDS, the limits and boundaries are based on terms like victims, incurable, terminal, death sentence, and the media feeding people a chronic diet of 'no hope.' AIDS is not a terminal disease unless we allow it to be. Healing begins when you want to live and start to take responsibility for your own life, and is a continuous process.

The first Sufi healing classes for AIDS, complementary to traditional medical care, began in January 1988. The AIDS patients meet for two hours twice a week. The Sufi Master has also worked personally with the participants very regularly to fortify their immune system through healing processes. One such process is by transmitting magnetic energies to them, regulating a balanced flow of energy throughout their body. "The healing of any wounds, physically and metaphysically, is based on acquiring a state of balance and equilibrium between the physical state of consciousness and the existential healing powers," says Hazrat Salaheddin Ali Nader Angha.

At this time the Master has given instructions for classes that the participants attend regularly every week where they are learning to recognize and work on their bodies' own healing abilities. As they recover they are seen less frequently by the Sufi Master, and become active participants in their own healing.

Sufi Healing covers a broad spectrum because it considers different aspects of the human being, which are: (1) Mental, (2) Physical, (3) Emotional, (4) Spiritual, (5) Nutritional, and (6) Energy fields of the body. Other approaches to healing do not focus on all these; only one or perhaps two or, at the most, three would be emphasized.

Sufi healing differs most remarkably in its focus on the spiritual and electromagnetic areas. It works extensively with energy, with the body's electromagnetic field, and with the energy centers in the body. Specific exercises designed for AIDS patients by the Sufi Masters are intended to provide a stable, balanced equilibrium in the magnetic functions of the body. Strengthening the energy sources and balancing the energy, combined with releasing stress and relieving pressure on the entire system has a profound effect on the stimulation of the immune system and the body's healing abilities.

The spiritual connection is also very essential. Sufi healing teaches the way within, and through personal experience one becomes aware of one's spiritual identity. One begins to experience the presence of God as one finds access to the healer within, and faith, hope and love begin to flourish. It is a healing process that generates love and self-worth and self-respect. "Life is born from the twilight of love" says Hazrat Salaheddin Nader Angha.

In a panel discussion on "The Art of Sufi Healing as Applied to AIDS," at California State University, Sacramento, on August 5, 1989, five AIDS patients who had been under the direct care of the Sufi Master consented to speak publicly about themselves.

Panelist A:

He had AIDS for two years. He told the panel that he had started attending the Sufi healing classes just after recovering from a near-fatal, week-long coma. He has since returned to college and is also working part-time, in spite of people questioning him. He is determined to live and enjoy life. His last T-4 cell count was 19 (under 500 is considered dangerous for opportunistic infection). Yet he has been healthy for the last year.

Panelist B:

He spoke of increased self-esteem, of new potential, and of feeling empowered. He stressed the fact that he was absolutely exhausted when he first came to class but was re-energized and revitalized when he left. His clogged sinuses had cleared and he experienced no more 2:00 a.m. panic attacks or dark days of despair and depression.

Panelist C:

Near tears, he had difficulty speaking. He told the public that he had attended the healing classes after two hospital bouts of 40 days each of cryptococcal meningitis, hallucinations, and fevers of up to 107 degrees. He thought he was dying and had lost 35 pounds, and was weak and in pain. Soon after undergoing healing instructions, his fungal count of 285 quickly subsided to less than 4, and he went from a wheelchair to walking again. His energy level has increased, his pain is reduced, and his outlook has become much more positive. He reduces the pain of spinal taps by meditating beforehand. He said that the Sufi healing had saved his life.

Panelist D:

He was introduced to Sufi healing in 1988, when he first tested positive for AIDS virus. Results of the classes were immediate, he said. He calmed down; he came to realize he was not just the body he was occupying, but that he also had a soul. He spoke of love, life, peace, and joy.

Panelist E:

He spoke with great emotion and was near tears. He had also attended the healing sessions for a year. He said that his medical history is on file and he did not wish to speak about it. After being quite ill, he was healthy again, and that was all that mattered. He had found an inner source of power and through it he was going to stay alive and happy. This is a summary of the panel discussion that took place, each patient talking about their process of recovery and renewed hope.

About hope the Sufi Master Hazrat Salaheddin says:

> Hope is seed that is cultivated in fertile soil, that bears fruit. In the land of our heart the plant of despair will never grow.[1]

"If you are an optimist by nature, then you are already halfway there," says Marlene Martin, free-lance writer who writes primarily on the subjects of health and nutrition, in an article named "Healing from Within." "Studies have shown," she continues,

> that people with a positive attitude toward life tend to get sick less often than pessimists. It is also believed by some that a positive attitude can in itself mobilize our immune systems. Psychologist David McClelland of Boston University's Center for Applied Sciences conducted studies in 1987 showing increased levels of salivary immunoglobulin A – an antibody that protects us from respiratory infection – in some people who exhibit strong feelings of love.[2]

Contrary to the Western medical tradition, in the East, due to the philosophy of life inherited from the great Sufi Masters and the knowledge of Sufism, diseases, even terminal ones, are not considered fatal. A patient who is terminally ill is often not even told so, for it is believed that the *morale* of the patient will weaken, and that he would lose faith and give in to the illness. The inherent hope and will to live is the most important factor in the healing and recovery process. One has to fight for life, and in many cases the result is victory. In the case of some cancer patients, physicians and researchers are also taking a closer look at numerous cases of "spontaneous remission" and they have found that many of these patients have maintained a positive outlook and a belief in their ability to overcome their disease. One possible conclusion from these findings, continues Marlene, could be that "with all other factors being relatively equal, a patient's state of mind can often be the deciding factor in his or her degree of recovery from illness; or, with a disease, even whether or not he or she survives."[3]

Sufism reminds us that man is created in the image of God and that he is the worthiest, richest, and wisest of all – if only he knew. Man is connected to the infinite power source of existence. Such a man, a creation of God's own image, is not subject to indigence and misery and confined to sorrow and despair.

> The delighted souls and the eyes that can see are in love with beauty, and their joy lies not in living in seclusion or living in deep corners of sorrow.[4]

CHAPTER ELEVEN ENDNOTES

1.   Salaheddin Ali Nader Angha, *The Secret Word*, UPA Publication, 1989, p. 20.

2.   *US Air Magazine*, article "Healing from Within," by Marlene Martin, Aug. 1990, p. 80.

3.   Ibid., p. 80.

4.   Shah Maghsoud Sadegh Angha, *The Message from the Soul*, p. 39.

CHAPTER TWELVE

INTRODUCTION TO MEDITATION

Both your pain and your cure
are from within yourself

Hazrat Ali-ibn-abitalib

In previous chapters we spoke of meditation theoretically. The next nine chapters will include more practical information on meditation and concentration as well as the physical and psychological bearings of stress and how we can recognize and eliminate those on our body and mind. However, I must remind readers that the theory of practice is still theory only, and although this book was meant at first for students already attending meditation classes who desired more theoretical information, I have decided to present publicly the practical aspects of meditation in a form that can be somewhat useful to all.

Obviously, attending actual classes, which are monitored very closely, is a much faster and surer way to attain this knowledge. In a field where so much misconception exists, guidance and supervision are very important factors.

I must also caution and remind each interested individual that if you do not know what meditation is you can be misled very easily; the more you know, the less you will risk getting lost or confused. Not every bus will take you home, not every signpost that reads "meditation" is going to teach you how to meditate and not misguide you.

If you want to learn physics, it is easy to choose a class. The basic physics course will be more or less the same in whichever college or university you attend. But when you want to learn something that has no standard for the material, no academic criterion, you have to rely on someone else's experience and trust they are going to teach you the right thing and not mislead you.

The right meditation class transforms and takes you through an inner evolution. True meditation connects you with reality and makes you aware of our fundamental unity with everything in the universe. It should be a journey of growth in which one passes from one state of awareness to another, moving gradually to deeper and deeper levels of one's being. Ultimately, one passes from the level in which one has the awareness "I am body" to the level in which one experiences "I am God."

This important transformation involves a new behavior and thought pattern, which are in more harmony with the inner self. The meditator needs to pattern himself after the mystical alchemist who seeks to transmute lead into gold. Meditation is the alchemy of human consciousness.

Effective meditation should always be evaluated in terms of enrichment and inner growth. However, it is perhaps more appealing for some to focus on beautiful images and colors instead of disciplining oneself to reach the harmony within. It is easier and more fun to pretend that a magical force is flowing up the spine than it is to struggle with forgiveness. It is more fun to close the eyes and dream and fabricate rather to work on mind control. It is simpler to concentrate on a straight posture than it is to create straight thoughts about one's self-deceptions. It is easier to imitate the "Sufi dance" than it is to forego the long sleepless nights of prayers and the self-denial that leads to the ecstasy and dance of the ascetic. It is easier to concentrate on positive vibrations and sounds rather than to find God within. It is more restful just to relax and let go of tension than it is to remove the psychological reactions that caused the tension in the first place.

Unfortunately, meditation, the core of religious practice, has become a mere profession to too many incompetent teachers and institutions that are all too often out just to make money. If you give your car to an incompetent mechanic who does not do a good job, it is only your car; but in matters that concern your soul and total well-being, you cannot afford to gamble. You have to know exactly what meditation is, what it will do for you, and which is the right class to take.

Before we can learn to meditate we need years of preparation in order to gain control over mind and body. It may start with simple relaxation but progresses to deep concentration, telepathy, healing, self-awareness, and, in its final stage, a union with God.

Contrary to the common view and most instruction available on the subject, the development of muscles (as according to yoga) is fine, but it is not a shapely body and developed muscles that will lead to heaven; rather, it is through the control of desires that one is led closer to the immaterial. As long as we are captives of the body, its desires, and the mind and its hallucinations, we are bound to our basic natural instincts – and prisoners we will remain.

Most meditation classes do not go beyond a mere training of the body, including relaxation techniques, muscle toning, and perhaps some concentration exercises. Why these classes are called meditation classes is open to speculation, since their emphasis is obviously physical. But man is not just a physical being; he is composed of mind, body, and spirit, capable of creating a harmony between the three – in meditation. This goes far beyond physical training, vegetarian diets, and repetitious words.

Freedom from bondage of the temporary and release from its limitations, like a bird that finally breaks away from its cage and is free to spread its wings and fly in infinite space, is the goal. A voyage and a holy pilgrimage from the temporary to the eternal, from the finite to the infinite, is the goal. A trip back home is the goal of meditation.

The meditation classes of *Maktab Tarighat Oveyssi* [MTO School of Sufism], prepares the way to this inner journey. The classes are designed to help students become aware of their inner abilities, and to grow in all aspects. These classes offer an extensive program of inner evolution. Based upon the teaching of the eminent Hazrat Ali-ibn-abitalib, the first Shiite Imam of Islam, in the 7th century, who claims: "Both your pain and your cure are from within yourself," MTO believes that the cure of each individual is within, just as the source of both happiness and grief is within.

The celestial man, who had become his own tyrant, fell from the quiet paradise into the abyss of illusion, the devil's temple, and moving back and forth across the flames of torment and contradictory desires, he began to mold his brutal existence.[1]

Man is born with the need for happiness and immortality. This natural inborn instinct will account for every effort and struggle in life. Although the same goal is shared by all, different approaches are chosen by each person. One will seek happiness in knowledge, another in wealth and rank, a third in solitude and withdrawal from society, some in pursuing chastity and forsaking earthly pleasures. There are still others who look for happiness in a quiet and secure way of living.

Gustav Velebon says, "Although the search for happiness is one principle we all agree on but the means of acquiring it is different to every eye." And in the teachings of Buddha we read, "Find prosperity within."

CHAPTER THIRTEEN

THE METHOD OF CONCENTRATION IN MEDITATION

As a fletcher makes straight his arrow, a wise man makes straight his trembling and unsteady thought, which is difficult to guard, difficult to hold back. A tamed mind brings happiness

The Budda

Let us start with the mind and experiment as we become a laboratory. From our childhood we have been taught to pay attention only to external elements but never to look within. Hence most of us have nearly lost the faculty of being in touch with ourselves. It is, therefore, very hard work to control the mind from constantly going outside, and to concentrate all its powers.

Let us take some time now to do a thought observation.

THOUGHT OBSERVATION

- Sit motionless or lie down on the floor and close your eyes.
- Just observe the stream of thought with passive awareness, like a spectator who must not interfere.
- Try not to make judgments or show surprise, anger, dismay, sorrow, or any other emotion.
- Just watch and observe.

It comes as a shock for the beginner to find what an unruly place one's mind is. As the new meditator turns within, he faces continuous mind chatter and ceaseless flashing images. I have come across many people who have become so trapped in the turmoil of their daily affairs that they have lost all control over their lives and the power to lead their thoughts in the direction they desire. They seem utterly helpless and confused.

Case History #1

I remember a student of mine, a young, beautiful girl of twenty-five, who came to class complaining of a severe lack of concentration. She said, "My biggest problem is that I cannot concentrate on anything. It is as if my thoughts are not my own. I cannot control them; they take me with them where they want to. Even when I engage myself in an activity that I really enjoy or pursue a goal I have chosen, I lose my concentration and my thoughts lead me to other subjects I have not chosen to think about. Believe me," she lamented, "I have come to the conclusion that these are not my thoughts!"

Now, do thoughts have a mind of their own? How can we have an action without a subject performing that action? My student was convinced she was not thinking; if that was so, then who was thinking? Can the "I," the subject, be missing or lost among the numerous flashing and distracting thoughts in one's mind?

In order to clarify this, an example in the Sufi discipline, "the chariot," will help explain. Let us consider a chariot and two horses, the power to pull the chariot. Let us imagine that the horses take off without a driver. Where will they go? Will they choose a specific route or goal? Do we not need a driver who knows the direction he wishes to go and is active and determined to keep the chariot moving in that particular direction? Now think of the chariot as the mind, the horses as power, and the driver as the active will. The three have to work together in order to avoid confusion. The driver, of course, has to be in command.

Concentration deals with mind-control. Tuning and training the mind as an athlete tunes and trains his body is one of the primary steps toward effective meditation. With special techniques we are able to work on the active will and to awaken that inner identity in order to take control of our undisciplined minds that refuse to obey the will. Saint Theresa of Avila once described the mind of man as an "unbroken horse" that would go anywhere except where it is bid.

Speaking of mind control, I also remember a science fiction movie about a computer that suddenly starts functioning by itself and refuses to obey the orders given by the computer operator, who was successfully working with it up to that critical moment. In this chaotic situation the computer starts to mix up all the data, gives out unwanted printouts, and becomes totally uncontrollable. While watching the movie I found many similarities between the wild computer and the uncontrolled human mind.

The mind can become confused for different reasons. One common reason is what I call the "Open House" syndrome. We have all seen "Open House: signs on houses that are for sale, and perhaps have visited some or even might have experienced having an "Open House" in our own home. There is a purpose for it, and that is to advertise to sell the house. Normally you would decide who came in to your house. But when you have an "Open House," the door is open and almost anyone is welcome. Similarly, when we eat, we try to eat food that is best for us that is fresh and nutritious; we watch what we eat. But when it comes to our mind, we let everything enter, without being selective and deciding if we need that information, what we are going to do with it, if it is nutritious, and if it is going to be enriching.

Our minds are open houses that accept and store almost anything that comes in and that never get cleaned or organized. When was the last time you sat down and thought about cleaning your mental household? Can you possibly imagine everything you have up there? Would you like to be living in a house that has a sign post saying "Open House." Think about it! If you could not control the traffic coming and going in and out of your house, would you still call it your house?

The following is a helpful concentration exercise.

Exercise 1:
- Lie down on the floor and make yourself comfortable.
- Totally relax your body.

certain *slowness* that lacked mental swiftness and that limited his concentration, hindering his learning process. Everything added together seemed to indicate that he had a learning disability, but in fact it was not a disability in the true sense of the word but a lack of mental exercise. Once I realized what his problem was I designed special concentrational and mental exercises for him, and soon his grades became better. He now has two years of successful studies behind him and is working toward a bachelor degree in business and is planning to continue in graduate school.

One of the exercises that I used was the following:

Exercise 2:

- Seat yourself in a comfortable position that you can maintain for a while.
- Place both hands in front of you on the floor: the palms of the hands should be down.
- Close your eyes.
- Imagine your right hand flat on the floor, also picture it in your mind.
- Now try and picture your right hand as if it were in front of your eyes. Picture the hand somewhere before your closed eyes and turn it around so that you see the back, the front, the sides, the tips of the fingers. Then put your hand down.
- Now focus your attention inside your head. Try to become aware of the area where your brain is and let your attention roam around in that space for a while.
- Become aware of the right hemisphere of the brain and then the left and the corpus callosum, the connection between the two sides; also note the convolutions of the brain.
- Become aware of all the activity in the brain, electrical activity as well as chemical activity. Feel how very active the brain is electrically and chemically. Focus all your attention there.
- Create the image of your right hand, as if the right hand is there in the brain. Make that image three dimensional.
- What is that three-dimensional image like? Is the hand stretched out or have you made a fist? What does it look like?
- Let the hand go away from the brain now and just feel both hands resting on the floor again, the palms down.
- Think about the connection between the hand and the brain. Focus on the brain and then focus upon the hand, and keep alternating your attention from one to the other.

- Breathe freely as you switch your awareness from one to the other. Does it seem more natural to breathe in as your attention moves up towards the brain and breathe out as your attention comes down toward the hand?

- Now practice doing it the opposite way, inhaling as your awareness moves down toward the hand and exhaling as your awareness rises toward the brain.

- Again try it the other way. Which is easier?

- Think about the right hand. Think about making a fist on the floor. Think about making a fist up in your brain.

- Imagine making a tight fist and then letting go, while your hand is resting on the floor; just imagine it and feel the sensation. Repeat this three times. What do you feel in your muscles when you imagine making a fist and then letting go of it?

- Try and feel what happens when you think about making a fist and when you release it. What do you feel in your wrist? in your arm? in your shoulders? Do you also sense it in the neck, eyes, mouth, or even in your breathing?

- Focus your attention in the brain area and give instruction to the hand to make a fist and then to release. As you do this become aware of the connection between the two. Feel that an impulse goes from the brain to the hand. The brain orders the hand to make fist; once the fist is made a signal returns to the brain letting it know that the fist is made. Although this whole process happens in a split second, try to feel this going-back-and-forth of the messages.

- Now, for the first time, make the fist with your right hand and let go and repeat this several times.

- See what you feel in your wrist, arm, neck, and face.

- Now feel your left hand. Feel both hands simultaneously.

- Sense the right side of your body and then the left side. Which side is clearer? Compare the sensing of the two sides.

- Lie down on your back for a moment, and observe how the two sides lie.

- Observe your breathing. Is the whole body breathing equally? Is it equal on both sides? How clear is the breathing on the left side?

- At this time imagine an image of yourself lying down.

- Examine this image from above and below and from the sides.

- Sit up again and focus on the brain. Now feel it with both hands. Feel the aliveness of the brain. Feel it pulsate and move. What does it sound like? Can you feel any electrical activity?

- Sense the outside of the head again, and the inside, and the brain, the left and the right hemisphere. Feel the ears and their connection to the brain; the sense of hearing and the sense of sight.

visible world of effects to the inner world of causes. No longer is he a mere puppet controlled by mass opinion but a co-worker with the forces of nature.

When we practice meditation, the mind goes deeper and deeper within and becomes more quiet. When it becomes clear, it is then able to touch its own source, becoming more and more a mirror to the light within. Like a pool whose surface, when ruffled by the winds of anger and desire, is unable to reflect the sun, the agitated mind can no longer mirror and reflect the truth. It is upon the serene and placid surface of the quiet mind that the visions gathered from the invisible find a representation in the visible world. In other words, inspiration cannot work through a turbulent instrument; the eye of wisdom cannot see clearly through the mists of sorrow and joy. The greatest happiness comes when one stills the mind. If the mind is weak and distracted, even the healthiest body becomes diseased. Minds tuned to the full reality are very different from narrow minds, trained to the practice of either/or, black or white, good or bad, high or low, functioning only by habit, and, in short, attempting to measure infinity with a yardstick.

As written in *The Dhammapada*,

> As a fletcher makes straight his arrow, a wise man makes straight his trembling and unsteady thought, which is difficult to guard, difficult to hold back. A tamed mind brings happiness.

> Irrigators lead water where they will; fletchers shape the arrow, carpenters shape wood to their will, wise men shape themselves.[1]

The true man's destiny is not shaped by his environment but by his own free will. The human being has the freedom to become anything. By his own power he can make his life sublime or wretched. By his own power he can reach the heavens or descend to the depths. For a person who is in touch and is in harmony with reality, even a dry desert is a celestial garden, even a prison is a wide-open space. But for one who does not know his own self and is out of touch with reality, even a celestial garden is like prison. And as Buddha says: "Showers of gold pieces will not satisfy the one who is in pain."

Control of the mind opens a new path to a higher realm of life. Spiritual development, however, is not possible without sound physical equipment, which will be the subject of the next few chapters.

CHAPTER THIRTEEN ENDNOTES

1. Buddha's Teachings, *The Dhammapada*, translated by Irving Babbit, New Directions Publishing Corporation, 80 Eighth Ave., New York 10011, p. 8.

CHAPTER FOURTEEN

ACHIEVING UNITY THROUGH PHYSICAL CONTROL AND AWARENESS

*Equilibrium and balance are the law
that should govern this unified being.*

Mental control is easily understood, but what is physical control? Is it to go without oxygen for a period of twenty-four hours? Or to survive on a single date a day? Or to sit on needles and not feel the pain? Or to develop incredible physical muscles in order to perform acrobatics?

Although the above feats, practiced by some yogis, require severe physical discipline and are by no means small achievements, these types of achievements are not the goals in the MTO, *Maktab Tarighat Oveyssi*, meditation classes. The health of the body and its overall balance, maintained by the right diet and sufficient exercise, is very important.

Some religious practitioners tend to trivialize the human body, regarding it as inferior, while considering the spirit to be superior. Others place importance only upon the physical body. Among all the misinformation about Islam, the principle of UNITY, its main principle, still survives. Islamic Sufism emphasizes theory of unity, which considers mind, body, and spirit as one; each represents only abstractions that try to separate aspects of a unified organism. So mind, body and soul are one complex unity. Object, use and user. The creator, the work and the audience, in each case, the unity, is what makes the meaning.

Therefore, in the Islamic discipline, there is no opposition between the spirit and flesh and between mind and matter but the view and principle is based on the multiple hierarchy of being and unity. This means that we cannot separate the body from the mind, nor either from the soul, because a human being is body, mind, and soul. Equilibrium and balance are the laws that should govern this unified being.

The human body is the most beautiful, wondrous creation of God. It is not inferior or evil. It must be cared for and taken care of. However, the goal of life is not just to maintain the body, as dear and beautiful as it is. The body should be taken care of because it is the mold for the life and soul within, the shell in which the pearl grows; without the shell, there would be no pearl.

"When health is absent, wisdom cannot reveal itself, art cannot manifest, strength cannot fight, wealth becomes useless, and intelligence cannot be applied," said Herophilus, physician to Alexander the Great.

This is how important the body and its health is, not for the sake of developing muscles and outer beauty alone. The beauty and the truth within also needs recognition and expression. Like a car that must be kept in optimum shape in order to best serve the driver, the body has to be maintained for this purpose. The purpose of a car is to take you to your destination, but a beautifully maintained car that is washed and polished and kept in perfect condition will be no more than a heap of metal, or at the most a beautiful object, unless it serves its purpose. To wash and polish it alone for the sake of mere beauty is not what the car is made for.

The Greek philosopher Socrates believed that the virtue of man is knowing and understanding his function; he uses the metaphor of the shoemaker: "If you want to be a good shoemaker," he said,

> the first thing necessary is to know what a shoe is and what it is meant for. It is no use trying to decide on the best sort of tools and material to use and the best methods of using them unless you have first formed in your mind a clear and detailed idea of what it is you are setting out to produce and what function it will have to perform. The virtue of a shoemaker depends first and foremost on the possession of this knowledge. He ought to be able to describe in clear terms the nature of the thing he intended to make, and his definition should include a statement of the use to which it was to be put. The first task,

therefore, if we are to acquire this universal human virtue, is to discover what the function of man is.[1]

Therefore, the goal of man is to reach his human potential and connect with his infinite source of knowledge and inner wealth so that he is *the image of God*. Man is then to acquire his true value. Man is to know himself, a self-recognition that goes beyond his body. "You think of yourself as a small mass (cluster) of matter, while within you lies the infinite existence,"[2] proclaims the eminent Imam Ali.

Therefore, the physical part of our training is only a starting point; it is not an end or the ultimate goal of our meditation classes, as it is in so many. Our awareness may start with the physical body but must gradually progress to more and more subtle parts of our being and go far beyond the body. Why become satisfied with a beautiful body? Why not aim for the beauty itself? And for eternal everlasting life, something that the body cannot provide.

However, the physical aspect of our training deals with strengthening the body, gaining control over the physiological process that enables one to control one's metabolism, to induce changes to treat psychosomatic ailments, to ease anxiety, control brain patterns, regulate the breath, and secure and maintain balance and physical health in the body.

The most important accomplishment of the "meditative therapies," such as autogenic training and progressive relaxation, is they make people aware they can have control over their autonomic or involuntary physiological functions. Voluntary control of the involuntary nervous system was considered impossible a decade ago. Once one begins to realize that this self-regulation can extend to all areas of one's life, one can change one's lifestyle in a more positive direction. Because of the importance of volition one becomes active and responsible in the process of the healing treatment rather than a passive victim of stress or disease.

In order to gain such control we need to increase our awareness about the body and how it functions. "Know Thyself," as the prophets said, starts with knowledge on a physical level.

PHYSICAL AWARENESS

- Right at this moment, which parts of your body are making contact with the chair or the floor?
- How deep is your breath?
- Is your body symmetrical?
- How do you feel your body?
- As you read this book, what noises can you hear?

All these questions have to do with our awareness. To sharpen our awareness is to increase our consciousness toward what is going on within and around us.

Awareness Exercise

- Have a sheet of paper and a pen available.
- Seat yourself quietly on the floor or on a chair.
- Close your eyes, and make sure you are comfortable.
- Ask yourself the following questions.
  What is happening right now?
  What am I thinking right now?
  How am I feeling?
  How am I breathing?
  What are my senses telling me?
  How clearly can I picture myself, and the way I am sitting?
- Slowly open your eyes now.

CHAPTER FOURTEEN ENDNOTES

1.   W. K. C. Guthrie, *The Greek Philosophers*, Harper Torch Books, London, 1950, p. 72.

2.   Hazrat Ali, *Nahjul Balagha*, translated by Seyd Mohammad Askari Jafery, P.O. Box 1115, Elmhurst, New York, 11373.

CHAPTER FIFTEEN

BUILDING BODILY BALANCE
AND PERFECT POSTURE

*Stress is one of the main
sources of bad posture.*

POSTURE

Our posture tells a lot about us. Poor posture can be caused by staying in one position for too long and sitting in bad posture in ill-designed furniture for long periods of time. This inactivity, together with increasing muscle tension from stress and other sources, is one of the main causes of bad posture.

Our posture is influenced by our mental and psychological well-being. Each person has a characteristic way of responding to stress by tensing particular parts of the body. Our bodies have become a storehouse of tension; when we contract certain muscles and create painful knots in response to tension, our posture reflects this.

It is very noticeable to me at the beginning of each class how my students walk in, many with one shoulder raised much higher than the other, crumpled toes, tight fists, and wrinkled faces. A noticeable difference is apparent at the end of class. However, if these contractions remain, in time tension builds up and affects our posture, causing abnormalities, limited motion, and damage to the nervous system. The first step is to recognize your body's particular signals.

Lower Back

The lower back is one of the most common problem areas and is highly susceptible to stress. Lower back and hip inactivity cause the spine to become very rigid and vulnerable. Ill-designed chairs that do not support the back and jobs that require a lot of standing or bending or lifting heavy objects cause bad posture and injury to the lower back.

Neck/Shoulders

Too much driving, keyboard work, and sitting in one position for too long cause tension in this area. It interferes with the circulation of the blood, causing "tension headaches." The shoulders, which can become tight and painful, are a common tension area in the body.

Face

Many people gather a lot of tension in the face area, which causes premature lines. The clenching of teeth and tight jaws is yet another source of headaches. It is incredible what a relaxed face does for you. I have a mirror handy in class because too often I need to ask students to look in the mirror to see how beautiful they have become after class is over. With all that worry and tension wiped away, faces become smooth, very radiant, and peaceful.

Chest

The tension and contraction in this area interferes with breathing deeply and can cause severe chest pains.

Stomach

Diseases of the digestive tract that are either caused or aggravated by stress include bloated stomach, gastritis, stomach and duodenal ulcers, ulcerative colitis, and irritable colon. For many people, this is the weak spot in the body and stress reaction shows up in this area.

Beautiful posture can be developed; corrections can be made once one is aware of the weaknesses and the abnormalities we have created. Poor posture affects your whole body, puts stress on your skeleton and internal organs, and damages your self-image. Make a posture check right now.

POSTURE CHECK

- Stand in front of a full-length mirror and check your posture.
- Is your head too far forward?
- Is your head too far back?
- Is your the chest too far forward?
- Is your chest dropped?
- Are your shoulders too far forward?
- Are your shoulders too far back?
- Is your back rounded?
- Is your back arched?
- Is your pelvis tilted forward?
- Is your pelvis tilted backward?
- Is your diaphragm low?
- Are your feet aligned?
- Is your body symmetrical?
- Are your pelvis, chest, head, and shoulders centered?
- Are your knees locked?

Standing with your body correctly aligned burns the fewest possible calories. The reason is that proper alignment allows the muscles in the front and the back to be used evenly. All your muscles work together to hold you up against gravity. When the body is aligned and the body parts are arranged correctly, you are allowing your muscles to function efficiently.

If your alignment is not correct then you will not move freely and your body will continuously be vulnerable to injury.

ALIGNMENT

What is correct body alignment? It helps to think of the body as being made of three principle parts: 1) The head; 2) the rib cage; and 3) the pelvis, all attached to the spine. They are also connected to and supported by two legs, which are balanced on top of the feet. When all these elements are correctly arranged and balanced, then the body is aligned.

- Start with the head, and hold it so your ears are over your shoulders.
- Proceed now to the rib cage. The rib cage needs to be directly above the pelvis, not leaning back or slumping forward.
- Now pay attention to your shoulders and make sure they are gently held down.
- Now align your pelvis. Your pelvis needs to hang down from your spine so that your back is a relaxed vertical line. It must not be tipped backward causing an exaggerated curve in the waistline, nor should it be tipped forward or tucked under so that the curve in the lower back diminishes. No extra muscular effort should be needed to keep the pelvis correctly aligned. Try unlocking the knees, which helps align both the pelvis and the rib cage.
- Align the feet now, pointing them straight ahead and not letting them go out to the sides. Balance your weight on the entire foot, not just the heel.
- Have you become aware of the weaknesses in your posture?
- Which parts of your body react most quickly to stress?

Posture Correction Exercise

Now that we have become aware of our posture problems and weaknesses, try to exaggerate and then correct them again. For example, if your head is too far forward, hold it very far forward, then back; then center it. Look at yourself in the mirror; notice how much better you look on center! Then close your eyes and try to actually feel the difference. Try to exaggerate each of your weaknesses and act in the same way.

- If your shoulders are too far forward, exaggerate by pulling them even more forward, and now back, and finally centering. Look at yourself in the mirror and admire your beautiful centered shoulders. Close your eyes and again feel the difference.
- If your shoulders are too far back, pull them back even farther, then pull them forward and now center.
- If the back is rounded, exaggerate that roundness. Now lengthen the spine to the point that you are arching your back. Now align and center.
- If the pelvis is tilted forward, try and tilt a little more, then tilt backward, and now unlock the knees and center and align the pelvis and the rib cage. Examine the correct posture in the mirror. Close your eyes and feel the difference.

In this way work on all the different areas that are irregular and need correction. Remember that awareness is the first step. You can take corrective measures only when you become aware of those weak points in the body, causing your posture to change completely in time.

PHYSICAL EXERCISE

The MTO physical therapeutic system corrects irregularities in posture motion and metabolism. Again, each person has a characteristic way of responding to mental tension by contracting and tensing particular parts of the body. Through time these tensions stimulate and affect the nervous system and the body in general. With the help of physical exercises, the body can be rid of any tensions and will regain its healthy, balanced and state. Among other benefits are regulation of the heartbeat, blood circulation and breathing. The regulation of breath results in the uniform distribution of oxygen throughout the body, which is essential to health.

Take an hour out of each day to relax, stretch, and release the tensions in the body. After physical and mental relaxation you will have much more energy, will feel much stronger and more concentrated. We have almost forgotten how to be naturally relaxed and in a worry-free state. Let us experience it again.

RELEASING TENSION

Interestingly enough, I have noticed in my classes that most people are not aware of the degree and amount of tension they experience in their bodies simply because they almost never relax. They are used to the pain and tensions stored in the body and carry it with them from day to day, hardly paying any attention to it.

In order to relax fully and to remember once again what it is like to be relaxed, try the following exercise, designed to contrast the way you feel when you exaggerate tensing your muscles with the way you feel when you relax them. This technique will leave you fully relaxed.

- Lie down on your back, and extend your legs out in front of you.

- Make sure that you are resting comfortably. Do not support your head unless you need to. Use a pillow under your knees if you are suffering from back pain.

- Let your arms fall to the side not touching your body.

- Close your eyes.

- Start to breath deeper, and see how you feel lighter as your breath becomes deeper.

- Breathe normally.

- Start with your feet and curl your toes very tightly, as tightly as you can. Hold this tension for a count of five, then relax.

- This time try to flex your feet, pulling your heels towards you, and again hold for a count of five, then relax.

- Now point your feet out away from you and hold for five and relax.

- Experience how relaxed the feet feel. Proceed from the feet to the rest of the body.

- Tighten the knees, almost raising the feet off the ground, holding the tension for a count of five, and then relaxing.

- Tighten the hips and hold that tension for a count of five; now release and relax.

- Pull in the abdomen and keep it in; after a count of five completely let go.

- Expand your chest, as if throwing it out in front of you, coming off of the ground a little; hold the tension and the breath, then release.

- Approach the shoulders now, raising the arms off the ground and tensing them quite tightly almost to the point of pain; after five counts you may let go completely. Feel the difference.

- Tighten the arms now, hold and relax.

- Make very tight fists with your hands.

- Spread the fingers outward and hold the tension for a count of five; as you let go and relax the fingers, notice how they feel.

- Try and reach your chest with your chin without raising your head off the ground.

- Roll your head back on the floor as far as possible, stretching out the neck. Relax and feel the difference.

- Open your mouth as wide as possible and keep it open for a count of five, then close.

- Press the teeth tightly together, clenching them. Hold, then release completely.

- Push the tongue as far back as possible toward the throat; try and hold for a count of five and then release and relax.

- Close your eyes tightly and hold the tension. Let go and close the eyes lightly.
- Raise the eyebrows toward the forehead as high as possible; as you let go notice the difference.
- Frown very fiercely, bringing the eyebrows as close to each other as possible. Let go of the tension in the face completely.

What you feel now is simply a natural state of the body; now you know how it should always feel. Just enjoy the freedom from tension. Go back to any areas of the body as needed.

EXERCISES TO DO ON THE JOB

It is best not to build up tension for long hours, but that can often happen at work. These are very helpful exercises that can be performed at work, especially if your job requires sitting for long hours, with occasional swiveling of the chair to reach for the file cabinet, computer, or telephone.

Exercise 1: Back Twist

- Sit in a chair with your knees and feet together; place the feet flat on the ground.
- Place your right hand on your left knee.
- Place your left hand on the back of the chair.
- Take a deep breath.
- Gently twist your upper body toward the left, looking over your left shoulder, as you start to exhale.
- Hold for five counts, breathing normally.
- Breathe in and gently return to the front as you exhale.
- Place your left hand on your right knee.
- Place your right hand on the back of the chair.
- Breathe in; as you start to exhale, twist the upper body to the right. Look over your right shoulder.
- Hold for five seconds.
- Return to the front very gently.
- Repeat three times on each side.

If it was easier for you to move to one side rather than the other, you might want to repeat the exercise and work on that particular side one more time.

Exercise II: The Forward Bend

- Sit with your hips touching the back of the chair.
- Place your feet flat on the floor. If your feet do not reach the floor put a book under them.
- As you breath in raise both arms high up in the air, extending them out in a wide V above your head.
- Lean forward as you are exhaling until your head hangs limply over your knees and your hands are loosely crossed on your feet.
- Relax for a few seconds.
- Raise the body very slowly back to the upright position.

Exercise III: The Knee Folding

- Sit on the edge of the chair.
- The feet should be flat on the floor.
- The arms should hang very loosely at your sides.
- Raise your right knee by clasping both hands round it and pulling it as far as possible toward the chest.
- Breathe in as you do so.
- Hold both the squeeze and the breath for five seconds.
- Start to breathe out while returning the leg to the floor.
- Now raise the opposite knee toward the chest and breathe in.
- Hold for five seconds and release and breathe out while returning the leg to the floor.
- Repeat three times on each side.

CHAPTER SIXTEEN

STRESS AWARENESS:
ELIMINATING BARRIERS TO SELF-KNOWLEDGE

You have to become aware of the
stress signals your body sends.

In this and the next chapter we will learn how to recognize the body's reactions to stress, and how to recover more quickly from the extra demands of life's stresses while at the same time learning to change responses to new and more positive ones.

MIND/BODY RELATIONSHIP

We said that each person has a characteristic way of responding to stress by tensing particular parts of the body. In this way, our physical posture reflects our physical and mental well-being. One cannot be separated from the other. We have to work on not just the effects and traces that stress leaves on our body but also the causes of stress.

It is incredible how the mind affects the body and how we tend to react to stressful situations by tensing our muscles. Most, if not all, muscular tension is self-produced.

Recently, I came across a very interesting case of a student suffering from asthma. She is a very intelligent and dedicated student who has been coming to meditation class for more than a year. She has been suffering from asthma for years. During the holy month of Ramadan we worked on a self-improvement program in which the students set important goals for themselves. This particular student approached me after class and said, "It may sound funny, but I am going to get rid of my asthma by the end of the month. I am almost sure I have brought this upon myself and therefore I can get rid of it, and I am tired of not being able to breathe." We talked a little about the history of her ailment and the medications involved. She was convinced that she could eliminate this problem, because she knew it was self-produced. She explained how her asthma had suddenly developed at a time when she was experiencing a lot of stress and difficulty in her life, and that she had absolutely no history of asthma before that stressful period in her life, a few years back. I encouraged her, although remembering the last attack she had in class made me wonder if she was going to succeed. She always brought her inhaler to class and had to use it on several occasions when she was completely out of breath. Yet before the month was over she was rid of her asthma for good; nearly a year has passed and fortunately she has not had a relapse.

What was happening in her case was that during times of stress, she contracted the muscles of her bronchial walls and therefore partial obstruction of the bronchi and bronchioles caused her attacks. She solved her long-lasting problem by learning proper breathing techniques and becoming aware that her problem was self-produced. I remember her saying, "If I was able to create such a problem, then I am able to get rid of it!"

In chapter seven we determined what stress was and the dangerous reactions it causes, from mild headaches to stroke, heart attacks to suicide. Let us start taking a positive step toward alleviating the "stress epidemic" that plays a large role in modern life.

First, pay close attention to the source of stress, become aware of our reactions, and how those affect the body. It is sad but true that most people are more aware of how their car functions than how their body does. We have a tendency to lose our sensitivity and awareness of our surroundings. The odors of strong chemicals in dry cleaner's or a printing shop, the sound of traffic, the harsh noise of heavy construction, the blare of loudspeakers, the constant ringing of the phone, the loud bell of an alarm clock have become part of our daily lives. People who work in environments with these and similar stressors often say, "Oh, I don't even notice it anymore." We become used to and ignore all kinds of stressors in addition to the ones mentioned; a disappointing job, or a relationship, or continual physical pain.

The following exercise will help us become more aware of what is going on around – and within – us.

Stress Awareness

- Write down the answers to the following questions on a sheet of paper.
- Write down as many sources of stress as possible that you experience each day, rating the frequency and the intensity of each one on a scale of 1 to 5.
- Write down some of the physiological effects of stress on your body.
- What are some of your physical problems?
- Could they also be stress related?
- Put your pen down for a while and look over your sources of stress.
- Close your eyes.
- What is it exactly that you want out of life?
- Think of the three major stressors in your life. Write these down.
- Evaluate the degree to which your reactions or behavior due to stress have helped you attain what you want.
- Determine whether you can eliminate your source of stress.
- What are some behavioral changes or alternative plans of action you need to develop to experience less stress?
- Do you find that you are becoming tense and feel physical discomfort as you are thinking about stressors? Do you feel some muscles tightening up as you are remembering them?
- Do you feel a particular group of muscles becoming tense? Pay attention to that particular area of your body.
- Where exactly is it?
- Turn the page now and look over the list of stressors and the related mental and physical indicators on the following pages. See if there is anything on these lists that you have left out and would like to add to your list.
- Add the new item or items to your list.
- Take a deep breath and try to relax now.

Some Sources of Stress

	Frequency	Intensity
	1 2 3 4 5	1 2 3 4 5

- Unclear purpose in life
- Choices
- Social acceptance
- Separation/Divorce
- Marriage
- Financial concerns/payments/debts
- Deadlines/Exams
- Rush jobs
- Health concerns
- Overcrowded living conditions
- Noise
- Relocating
- Neighbors/Neighborhood
- Responsibilities
- Expectations/Demands (home, social)
- Recent death in the family
- Relationships
- Traffic
- Current events
- Phobias
- Competition
- Self-demand
- Promotion
- Lay-off
- Physical appearance
- Loneliness
- Boredom
- Habits
- Weight problem
- Illness

- Smoking
- Alcohol
- Drugs
- Sex

Some Mental and Psychological Indicators

	Frequency 1 2 3 4 5	Intensity 1 2 3 4 5

- Increased irritability
- Lack of patience
- Nervous mannerisms
- Forgetfulness
- Depression
- Disappointment
- Anxiety for no apparent reason
- Lack of concentration
- Frustration/Anger
- Lowered Mental Activity
- Nightmares
- Helplessness
- Low self-esteem
- Negativity
- Mood swings

Some Physiological Indicators

	Frequency 1 2 3 4 5	Intensity 1 2 3 4 5

- Muscular pain
- Digestive difficulties
- Skin eruptions/pimples
- Stomach pain
- Heartburn
- Chest pains
- Grinding of teeth
- Headaches
- Back pain
- Constant fatigue
- Excessive sweating
- Shortness of breath
- High blood pressure
- Hyperactivity
- Irregularity of menstrual period
- Nausea
- Insomnia
- Eating disorders
- Constipation
- Exhaustion

However, it is not just negative situations that cause stress; stress can also be positive. A wedding is an example of a positive stress; another might be moving to a new home or even going on a trip or vacation, something you have been planning and waiting for for a long time. These and other similar events can cause the same stress reactions. The body does not distinguish between "negative stress" and "positive stress" but considers all stressors as demands on the body and mind and the energy level. It does not even distinguish between an existing source of stress or the memory of one. Many times, after a stressful situation has passed, one seems to hold on to the stress reactions known as "stress momentum." These stress "ghost-like" reactions serve no purpose except to add more wear and tear on our bodies and waste our energy.

In order to make the body more stress-resistant, you must learn to communicate with your body and become aware of the stress signals it sends.

CHAPTER SEVENTEEN

STRESS AND ALTERNATIVE COPING STRATEGIES

*Man is not disturbed by events
but the view he takes of them.*

Epictetus

Life is never free from stress, but often each individual feels that he or she has a bigger share than everyone else! However, our next-door neighbors also get stressed, but it may be caused by different things or they may have varied reactions to stress. Or it could even be that they have learned some technique to help them cope with it. Is there a way we can cope with stress? And, if so, what is it?

It is definitely true that stress has less negative effects on some people because of their outlook on and philosophy of life. They have learned that by maintaining their health and strength and by adjusting the way they think, they can view life's stresses as challenges and opportunities to learn and grow from. Such people do not meet every stressful situation or unexpected event with sudden outbursts of anger, disappointment, or despair. This means less damage overall, and less time and effort for the body to recover from a stressful situation. Therefore, if there is absolutely nothing we can do to reduce the amount of stress in our lives, perhaps we should start thinking about changing our reactions to stress. We have a choice!

As part of the Personal-Growth program of the meditation classes that I mentioned earlier, I remember giving to a class an exercise that called for finding new solutions to old problems. At first the students were astonished. "If I could resolve my problem, don't you think I would have done so by now?" said a confident young man in his late twenties, a student of acupuncture. However, as difficult as it is looking at old problems from a new and different perspective, most people looked for alternative ways of dealing with their problems and some were even successful. The young man who had made the remark did not make an effort however, but another student reported later, "Yes, with a little patience and desire, one can seek and find new solutions, new answers to old problems."

One of the students who was having a problem with a co-worker complained the person would go out of her way to create problems for her and wanted to aggravate and upset her for no reason. For the first time she tried looking at the problem differently and changing her reaction toward the particular person. One day she came to class very happy and told the class how she *had* dealt with the co-worker and about her *new* approach. She said, "I thought to myself perhaps she just needed my attention and that she had nothing against me. And this was definitely the right answer. I tried to pay more attention and be nice to her and now the problem is over, we are even friends now!"

Therefore, we can start to make new choices and approach problems in different ways. We can become more positive and start gaining more control over our lives so that we start to run the show instead of the show running us.

I remember another student, a young man in his thirties, who complained about being very negative. He said, "Everyone complains about me being negative. It seems I look for the negative side of everything. How can I change myself? With this attitude I cannot achieve anything. I am even tired of hearing myself nag!"

After I reviewed his case history and we talked for a few sessions, I was able to trace the source of his problem to a particular stage in his life when several mishaps had occurred. After that he had started developing a new outlook, a negative one, which had become worse throughout the years. As he had practiced negativity more and more he became very good at it!

I helped him broaden his perspective as we worked together. During the course of the meditation classes, he gradually learned to widen his perspectives, and not to continue to look at everything from the exact same angle. He tried to be more flexible in his opinions and to accept certain situations, to be less critical and less judgmental. It was not easy for him to unlearn and change, but he knew that he hated the turn his life had taken and that he must do something before it was too late. Having to deal with an old problem is far more difficult than trying to solve matters as they happen. This, however, takes a bit of practice and a little more courage and strength, but is sure worth it in the long run.

As a wise uncle said to me once, after suffering the loss of a member of his family,

> We have two kinds of problems. The first is one that we can do something about, and the second is one that we can do absolutely nothing about, as in the case of my recent loss. We must try to distinguish between the two in order to save our energy for coping with the problems we can do something about. We must try to lower our expectation of others to the very minimum, the less the better, and the less one gets hurt.

It does not matter how wise we are however, we might eventually become hurt, betrayed, or feel bad in some way. Feelings such as fear, anger, guilt, and anxiety, if not dealt with in the proper manner, will create inner obstacles for us. They could limit or even paralyze us in some extreme cases. These become built-in excuses that literally stop us from getting what we want out of life and they interfere with our success in life. We start getting caught up and entangled in our feelings which usually evolve in a vicious circle :

```
..............I am angry...........................I react.............................
..............I react...................................I feel guilty......................
..............I feel guilty .......................I make excuses ...............
..............I make excuses...................I deny...............................
..............I deny...................................I am confused...............
..............I am confused....................I am exhausted...............
..............I am exhausted...................I am depressed...............
```

This is why that although a relaxation exercise can be very helpful, it is a temporary relief to the real problems. Our lives and the problems we encounter might be compared to the example of a runner; imagine a runner, running through the path of life. He starts out light and energetic, but every step down the road he picks up an extra load here and there, and as he proceeds he becomes heavier and heavier. It is good and necessary for him to take a rest but it give him only temporary relief. Wouldn't it be better if he put down the load he is carrying with him?

The power of memories and expectations is such that for most of us the past and the future are much more real than the present. The present cannot be lived happily unless the past has been "cleared up" and the future is bright with promise. The loads that we carry from the past and our expectations of the future could become inner obstacles.

The self-made inner obstacles inhibit the relaxed natural state of a person functioning with optimum energy. It stops us from going to where we want to go. We have to stop fighting with ourselves and realize that there is enormous human potential in us, a gift in every one of us that needs to develop and grow once we stop limiting and restricting and labeling everything as good and bad. We are too judgmental of ourselves. We are raised in a society in which we are taught early that events that happen to us do so because we are either "good" or "bad." In this way we are constantly looking to label ourselves, analyzing situations in this way.

The Sufi master Hazrat Salaheddin Ali Nader Angha teaches us that we must not look at events as "bad" but rather as experiences that we can learn from in order to become more mature. The importance of a past event is what we have learned from it to utilize for a better future. Actually, our loss is not because of what happened but rather at spending the precious time that we have, the present, to feel sorry for what happened in the past.

Life is full of such experiences that we can learn and grow from, instead of condemning ourselves and taking every event so personally. Feelings are feelings, accept it, it is natural – don't be depressed about being depressed. Don't be angry about being angry. Don't fear fear. These are feelings, experience them, and continue.

It is as if these feelings are the driving forces behind a boat. All the forces that you thought were against you are like current and winds; use them as a force to push forward as the wind and the water helps the boat move toward the designated goal. What you label as a "bad event," a "loss," a "failure" is an experience for you; use it and grow because of it. In fact it depends on how you interpret it. Two people might experience the same event, such as a loss of a business. However, one might consider it a personal failure while the other will say, "It's too bad," and go on to what he wants to do next.

"Man is not disturbed by events, but by the view he takes of them," says Epictetus. Give it a try, try a new interpretation, take a new picture, and look at it differently. Try to look at the positive side of it.

CHAPTER EIGHTEEN

RELAXATION:
EXISTENCE BETWEEN THOUGHTS

Relaxation is the ability to go beyond thought, time, space, reaching a moment of inner peace and quiet; in fact, reaching a moment between two thoughts.

What is relaxation? Take a moment and think about the things you do in order to relax. Was your answer, "Watch TV," or "Go to the movies," or "Have a drink," or even "Go to the beach," or "Read a book"?

However, relaxation is not an occupation such as reading a book, watching TV, or drinking alcohol but quieting the body and the mind. Relaxation is total stillness. It is the ability to go beyond thought, time, and space, reaching a moment of inner peace and quiet; in fact, reaching a moment between two thoughts.

Relaxation can only take place when the mind and the body are still, when the brain rhythm changes from an alert beta to a relaxed alpha rhythm. At this time a chemical associated with anxiety decrease and blood flow to the muscles declines; instead, blood flows to the brain and skin, producing a feeling of warmth and calm.

Relaxation is known to decrease high blood pressure and otherwise counteract the debilitating, health-draining effects of chronic stress – the frequent "fight or flight" response, the opposite-of-relaxation response, which is activated in the face of threat. It starts when the brain receives and interprets environmental signals that indicate danger. The nervous system responds by secreting hormones to mobilize the body's muscles and organs for defense. The messenger hormones carry this "red alert" signal throughout the body, triggering specific reactions including increased heartbeats, higher blood pressure, and faster pulse rates. The blood sugar increases (drawn from available proteins first, and then from storage) to provide instant energy if required. Calcium and other minerals are drawn from the bones to stimulate muscles in case the body has to move quickly. Body functions that are not absolutely necessary to meet this crisis (such as digestion) tend to slow down. Sodium content and thus water retention increase to prevent dehydration. All this happens in a split second. The body is now primed to face its attacker or flee. Of course, most of the time, there is no attacker but simply the everyday worries and pressures of modern life. Nevertheless, the body does not distinguish between a physical threat or an emotional or mental one; it reacts exactly the same way.

After the attack of stress and the alarm reaction, then the next stage is resistance, as defined by Hans Selye, mentioned in chapter two of this book. This is when the "threat" is removed and the alarm is over; the body goes into the stage of resistance, during which it starts to repair any damage and continues its various functions. Protein, once it has been broken down to provide sugar for energy, cannot be used again as protein; the lost minerals and other vitamins have to be replaced; nutrition must also be replaced. Both the mind and the body need to relax.

LEARN TO RELAX

How many times have you regretted a reaction you showed in a stressful incident, realizing afterward that you had overreacted and that it was not so serious or important? Does this show that our thinking patterns change when once under stress, as if our mind reverts to a more primitive, reactive state, judging only in terms of survival?

A stressed person feels constantly anxious and exhausted, and is very easily aggravated. His vision becomes narrow and becomes less effective. When he dreams he has nightmares; he may have difficulty falling asleep or waking up and usually gets out of bed feeling tired and unrefreshed.

Insomnia and fatigue are consistently associated with stress, and nearly all mental patients' problems are complicated by sleep disorders. As much as physicians try to help the patient sleep, the prescribed sleeping pills are a mixed blessing; and apart from the fact of being addictive they interfere with the ability to dream, a necessary component of successful rest.

Learning to relax is the first positive step away from overreacting to stressful situations. Relaxation does not happen spontaneously, but must be learned. It has been clinically proven that the effects of relaxation are vastly different from those of tranquilizers, alcohol, and other drugs. Patients with problems ranging from cardiovascular disorders to ulcers and allergies are constantly advised by their physician to relax, but are seldom instructed how to relax.

GIVE YOURSELF A BREAK

A temporary halt of mental activity is the best kind of relaxation. As soon as mental activity begins, relaxation ends. Sometimes there are so many things crowding your mental household that the mind becomes confused and anxious because it cannot make the right decisions and it becomes "blocked." Try drawing back from everything now for a few minutes, and give yourself a break! After these few minutes of mental relaxation, everything will become much clearer. Your mind will become more alert, refreshed, and even creative, and you will be able to tackle your problem with much more energy.

A Natural Break

- Locate a quiet place where you won't be interrupted.

- Wash your feet, face, and hands with lukewarm water, or at least sprinkle a little water on your face.

- Sit cross-legged and get yourself as comfortable as possible.

- Hands should rest comfortably on your lap.

- The eyes must be closed and remain closed during this time.

- Start breathing deeper and fuller.

- Concentrate on the sound of your breath as you breathe in and breathe out smoothly and evenly.

- Pay attention to your feet. Try to feel them and then relax them.

- Pay attention to your legs now and consciously relax them.

- How does your stomach feel? Try to relax it completely.

- Now relax your chest and once again pay attention to your breathing.

- Feel your shoulders, arms, and hands and relax them.

- Feel your neck and relax it.

- Feel your head and relax it.

- Pay attention to your face now and try to relax it.

- Pay special attention to the tiny muscles around the eyes and try to relax them.

- Relax the area around the temples.

- Make sure your teeth are not clenched and relax the muscles of your jaw.

- Where else do you feel tension? Relax it.

- Relax the whole body (although take care not to slouch and keep the back straight).

This will only take a few minutes, maybe as long as a coffee break, but the effects will be very different from sipping a cup of coffee, or smoking a cigarette, or drinking alcohol, or snacking on a candy bar because these are enemies of a stress-resistant diet. Try this natural break! Also try a natural "happy hour" after work. It will refresh and energize you and have a much more permanent as well as positive effect.

CHAPTER NINETEEN

THE HIDDEN AND INNER SOURCE OF STRESS

We know life only by its symptoms.

Albert Szent-Gyorgyi (discoverer of vitamin C)

Beyond the external stressors that play such a big part in stress, there is an inner source of stress that is often completely overlooked. When there is an obvious cause of stress, such as a having a deadline to meet, it is very apparent and easy to spot. However, when one feels stressed for no apparent reason, then what is the reason?

At the beginning of my career, I became acquainted with a young graduate student, a very hard-working and exceptionally bright individual who was teaching at the university and completing her studies at the same time. She was under a lot of stress and talked to me mostly about the physical symptoms she was having. These included severe digestion problems, loss of weight, lack of appetite, and a generally unhealthy appearance (as if she were suffering from malnutrition).

At first glance, it seemed to me to be a typical case of "the achiever's stress" and overwork; with a little relaxation, all would be well. I encouraged her to join a stress-management class I was teaching. She signed up and as I got to know her better, other symptoms started to surface, making me realize this was not a case of severe fatigue and overwork but an inner stress and deficiency. She complained, "Although I have been blessed with everything that a person might want to achieve in life – a good education and no major problems – I feel as if I am choking from within." She described her feelings of helplessness and frustration about not finding answers to her most basic questions. She could not understand and accept the fact that without knowing "why" she had to follow the norm and a certain pre-set pattern in life. She understood that to live in society one had to follow some rules and regulations, but where was life going in general? "What is the point of doing what I am doing? What is the end? Should my goal be to get married and have children and a stable job? Is this all I'm good for, and why should I do these things because everyone else does them? What is the purpose of being?" she would ask with an unimaginable expression of pain in her voice.

Later, I heard other students voice the same confusions and the frustrations about not understanding the purpose of life in general and therefore not being able to value their own lives. This lack of self-value might have much to do with the many problems that plague modern youths, including a high suicide rate and drug and alcohol abuse. Could it be that they might be asking the same questions as my graduate student?

"We know life only by its symptoms,"[1] says Albert Szent-Gyorgyi, meaning life has not yet been defined. "What is life, what is death?" "Will physical death put an end to our existence?" "Was I born just to live and die, or is there a higher purpose that I could attain in life?" "Who am I?" These are questions that preoccupy the minds of youth; perhaps because they can not find these answers is the reason they fly into fury, rage, and revolt. What is the purpose of their lives? What should they stand for? What is their value? principle? function?

The novel *Nausea*, by Jean Paul Sartre, the 20th-century French philosopher, describes the feeling of nausea that Sartre feels when he sees that everything stands for some reason and function, everything but himself. Even a doorknob creates feelings of nausea for him, because even the doorknob serves a function.

Many feel a similar inner stress but cannot voice their confusion and therefore sometimes harm themselves or others. Therefore, to try and treat only the effects of stress is to look at the problem very superficially, because the cause of the problem has to be taken care of.

Physicians are dedicated to the treatment of the body; psychiatrists and psychologists are concerned with healing the mind and emotions, while a third group, the clergy, attends the soul and spiritual healing. For the causes of inner stress, a healing process is required that involves the whole person, not just a part.

The traditional Eastern healing practice thinks of the mind and body functioning as an integrated unit; health exists when they are in harmony and illness results when stress and conflict disrupt this harmony. These healing approaches are essentially humanistic and re-establish an emphasis on the person and his or her healing potential, rather than on medical technology.

Dr. Robert O. Becker notes that since the discovery of penicillin in 1929, medicine changed face drastically. "Before then, medicine had been an art," he says.

> The masterpiece – a cure – resulted from the patient's will combined with the physician's intuition and skill in using remedies culled from millennia of observant trial and error. In the last two centuries medicine has come more and more to be a science, or more accurately, the application of one science, namely biochemistry. Medical techniques have come to be tested as much against current concepts in biochemistry as against their empirical results. Techniques that don't fit such chemical concepts – even if they seem to work – have been abandoned as pseudoscientific or downright fraudulent.
>   At the same time and as part of the same process, life itself came to be defined as a purely chemical phenomenon. Attempts to find a soul, a vital spark, a subtle something that set living matter apart from the non-living, had failed.[2]

Erwin Chargaff, the biochemist who discovered base pairing in DNA and thus opened the way for understanding gene structure, said this about biology: "No other science deals in its very name with a subject that it cannot define."[3]

What is life and its purpose? In Part Three of this book, we will look at some answers from the school of Islamic Sufism, since Sufism is concerned with such humanistic questions concerning values, purpose, self-identity, self-knowledge, and God-awareness.

PART THREE

CHAPTER TWENTY

ISLAMIC SUFISM

Keep watch over thy heart.

Hazrat Oveyss Gharani

Although the term Islamic Sufism or Sufism, has been mentioned throughout the text, it has not been defined yet. Sufism and Islam cannot be separated, which various dictionary definitions of the terms confirm. However, this does not mean that every Muslim is a Sufi, but it does mean that every Sufi is a Muslim. This will be explained in later chapters.

Let us consider some dictionary definitions of Sufism.

Root: from Arabic – suf, meaning wool

- *The Word Book Dictionary*:

  Sufi: A sect of Muslim mystics and ascetics, largely in Persia, today Iran, that originated in Islam.

  Sufism: Mystical system of the Sufi, using a symbolism popular with Muslim poets.

- *Encyclopedia International*:

  A phase of Muslim spiritual life, Sufism is centered on mystical religious experience.

- *The Dictionary of Religions*:

  The Sufis (wearers of wool, i.e., the coarse garments of the ascetic) are the Mystics of Islam.

- *The Encyclopedia of Philosophy*:

  Sufi is applied to Muslim mystics who, as a means of achieving union with Allah, adopted ascetic practices, including the wearing of garments made of coarse wool (suf).

- *The Random House Dictionary of English Language*:

  Sufi   1)   A member of an ascetic mystical Muslim sect.

             2)   Of or pertaining to Sufis or Sufism.

- *Encyclopedia of Religion and Ethics*:

  The terms "Sufi" and "Sufism" are to be understood in their ordinary sense, as equivalent to Muhammadan mystic and Mohammadan mysticism. Ancient Sufism had strong ascetic tendencies, while the mystical element might be insignificant; and there have always been Sufis of an ascetic and devotional type whom we should hesitate to describe as mystics in the proper meaning of the word.

THE HISTORY OF THE HOLY CLOAK

"The habit of wearing wool next to the skin dates back to the first Saints and Imams of Islamic Sufism. They believed that physical bodily comfort would encourage spiritual lethargy; that the spirit, not the body, should be in command at all times, and that the body should therefore be kept in a state of submission and obedience to the spirit."[1] It is said that one of the Saints or Imams of Islam once wore a silk garment. He was questioned by a student as to why he who renounces the world and its comfort was dressed in silk. His Eminence replied "This garment of silk, I wear for your sake, but," he said, pointing to a very coarse wool garment he was wearing underneath the silk next to his skin, "this, I wear for the sake of myself."

The Sufi is famous, however, for wearing a wool cloak. Although many have imitated this outer appearance of the Sufi, the cloak, Hazrat Mir Ghotbeddin Mohammad Angha, the 40th spiritual guide or *pir* of the Oveyssi School of Sufism, says, "While every Sufi wears wool, not every person who wears wool or *suf* is a Sufi."

This cloak of wool is symbolic of the spiritual knowledge and instruction handed down from one *pir* to another throughout the ages. The one who receives the holy cloak, as a result attaining a high degree of knowledge, is the one who receives permission to teach and guide. It is possible that a learned man may have had several masters, but acquires permission to guide from only one, and receives the cloak from that particular master and teacher. However, some masters possessed such a high degree of spiritual knowledge that each of the Sufi grand masters, not just one, granted them permission to guide the people. In this case, a particular master or *pir* received the cloak from the hand of each and every one of the saints and masters. When this happens different existing sects of Sufism join together under one name. This has been repeated several times in the history of Islamic Sufism, and thus the school takes the name of that particular master.

Why the Oveyssi School of Sufism?

The holy cloak is originally known to have been passed for generations from the prophet Abraham to the prophet Mohammad, then to Oveyss Gharani and other learned and enlightened teachers thereafter. Hence the Oveyssi school of Sufism Maktab Tarighat Oveyssi [MTO] is named after Oveyss Gharani.

Jalaledin Rumi *Molavi*, the famous Iranian Sufi poet, also joins Oveyssi's school from two different sects; on his father's side Bahaedin Valad, who was a disciple of the famous Sufi Najmedin Kobra, and his beloved master Shams Tabrizi, who himself was a disciple of Baba-Kamal Jondi, who, in turn was the disciple of Sheikh Najmedin Kobra Oveyssi.

In the famous book of poetry, *Massna*vi, by Jalaledin Rumi, we find this by the prophet Mohammad about Oveyss Gharani:
The Prophet Mohammad says,

> The breeze brings O'men!
> The divine perfume from Yemen.
>
> The scent of Ramin comes from Veyss,
> The fragrance of God from Oveyss.
>
> Oveyss's heavenly perfume from God,
> Overjoyed the heart of the prophet of God.
>
> Forsaking his mortal being willingly
> That earthly (Oveyss) become heavenly.[2]

Shams-din Hafiz Shirazi, another well-known Iranian Sufi poet with a worldwide reputation who has inspired great philosophers and poets all over the world and who is much admired, especially by the German philosopher Goethe, also was a member of the Oveyssi sect. He was the disciple of Sheikh Mahmoud Attar Shirazi, who was the disciple of *pir* Golrang.

The story of Oveyss Gharani's life and his absolute adoration for God is the subject of much poetry and commentary by the great masters of Sufism.

The instructions of the Oveyssi School of Sufism, Maktab Tarighat Oveyssi, are based on inward enlightenment and pure knowledge, indicating that to get to the truth, there is but one gateway: through the heart. Oveyss Gharani says, "Keep watch over thy heart," in Arabic, *alayka bi-ghalbika*, i.e., "Guard thy heart from thoughts of other." This saying has two meanings: 1)

Make thy heart obedient to God by renunciation, and 2) Make thyself obedient to thy heart.

While Oveyss Gharani never actually visited or set eyes on his spiritual teacher Hazrat Mohammad, he knew him in his heart, even more than those who had lived with Mohammad and seen, conversed, and received instructions from him in the traditional oral manner, conventionally called "seeing and hearing." This inner and spiritual relationship is the kind of relationship that should exist between the seeker and the teacher in Sufism. Let us hear how Oveyss explains such a relationship in his own words. It is narrated that a seeker of God, Harim b. Hayyan, went to visit Oveyss and before he had time to introduce himself, Oveyss said, "Peace be with thee, O Harim ibn. Hayyan!" Harim cried, "How did you know that I am Harim?" Oveyss answered. "My spirit knew thy spirit."[3]

The heart thus has the means of hearing and perceiving in an unlimited sense, strange as it may sound to the new-comer to the Sufi path. Such is the Oveyssi way, *tarighat Oveyssi*.

God will reveal his messenger to whom he wishes in this manner, and that obedient servant of God and the seeker of truth will know him only through his heart. In the Old and New Testaments and the Koran we repeatedly encounter verses that say it is by the grace of the Almighty and through the heart that one is able to know the truth.

In the Old Testament, Solomon says:

Keep your heart with all vigilance; for from it flow the springs of life.
(Proverbs 4:23)

But even yet the Lord hasn't given you hearts that understand, or eyes that see, or ears that hear.
(Deuteronomy 29:10)

We read in the Bible:

All things have been committed to me by my father. No one knows who the son is except the father, and no one knows who the father is except the son and to those to whom the son chooses to reveal him.
(Luke 10:22)

Such a revelation does not take place anywhere but in the heart of the pure.

Blessed are the pure in heart for they shall see God.

(Matthew 5:8)

The Koran says:

We have sent on to you a Messenger from you,
Who will read to you Our Revelations.
And will teach you the Knowledge of The 'Book,' and Wisdom.
And will teach you that of which you have no knowledge.

(2:151)

Yet those who do not witness the truth are described in the Koran as having sealed hearts: "Thus God seals the hearts of those who understand not."

(30:59)

When the truth has to be witnessed from within, there can be no false prophets. "The heart doubts not what it sees," says the Koran, and the Bible also warns us against false prophets. "And many false prophets will appear and deceive many people."

(Matthew 24:11)

Oveyss Gharani merited Abraham's holy cloak from the prophet Mohammad for his method of discovering and witnessing "the Inner Truth." Oveyss Gharani passed his cloak on to Salman Farsi, who was Persian. The prophet was very fond of him, "Salmam is one of us," said the prophet Mohammad praising him. From that time until the present over a period of 1400 years, the cloak has been in the possession of forty-two Sufis in unbroken succession. The present cloak-bearer and teacher of the same school and principles is Hazrat Salaheddin Ali Nader Shah Angha Pir Tarighat Oveyssi.

It is these great men who have had a mission to fulfill and a great message to convey and who have been the shapers of human dignity, the physicians of the soul, and the loudspeakers of truth. These great souls are in total harmony with the essence of nature. Divine guidance, self-discipline, ceaseless prayers, and continual service to mankind have opened their souls to the grace of Heaven, made their hearts the source of life, and their tongues the instruments through which the "Angelic Voice" of truth speaks. The pure and enlightened souls, transformed by the Great All-Knowing and Wise Alchemist, are however, but guides. They can but call upon men and convey the "Message of Truth," but may not guide against man's will, for only God can guide.

God thus spoke to Mohammad, his messenger, as recorded in the Koran,

> You may not guide whom you wish;
> I shall guide whom I wish to guide.
> Surah 28:56

Each heart must experience and hear the "Angelic Voice" and find his messenger within the innermost part of his being, the heart.

Genealogy of the School of Islamic Sufism

Maktab   Tarighat   Oveyssi   Shah Maghsoudi

PROPHET MOHAMMAD

IMAM ALI

1. Hazrat Oveyss Gharani
2. Hazrat Salman Farsi
3. Hazrat Abu Salim Habib-ibn Moussa Zeyd Rai
4. Hazrat Soltan Ebrahim Adham
5. Hazrat Abu Ali Shaghigh Balkhi
6. Hazrat Sheikh Abu Torab Nakhshabi
7. Hazrat Sheikh Abi Amr Estakhri
8. Hazrat Abu Ja'far Hazza
9. Hazrat Sheikh Kabir Abu Abdollah Mohammad-ibn Khafif Shirazi
10. Hazrat Sheikh Hossein Akkar
11. Hazrat Sheikh Morshed Abu-Eshagh Shahriar Kazerouni
12. Hazrat Khatib Abolfath Abolghassem Abdolkarim
13. Hazrat Ali-ibn Hassan Salebeh Bassri
14. Hazrat Serajeddin Abolfath Mahmoud-ibn Mahmoudi Sabouni Beyzavi
15. Hazrat Sheikh Abu Abdollah Rouzbehan Baghali Shirazi
16. Hazrat Sheikh Najmeddin Tamat-al Kobra Khivaghi
17. Hazrat Sheikh Ali Lala Ghaznavi
18. Hazrat Sheikh Ahmad Zaker Jowzeghani
19. Hazrat Noureddin Abdolrahman Esfarayeni
20. Hazrat Sheikh Rokneddin Alaodowleh Semnani
21. Hazrat Mahmoud Mazdaghani
22. Hazrat Amir Seyyed Ali Hamedani
23. Hazrat Sheikh Ahmad Khatlani
24. Hazrat Seyyed Mohammad Abdollah Ghatifi-al Hassavi Nourbakhsh
25. Hazrat Shah Ghassem Feyzbakhsh
26. Hazrat Hossein Abarghoui Janbakhsh
27. Hazrat Darvish Malek Ali Joveyni
28. Hazrat Darvish Ali Sodeyri

29.   Hazrat Darvish Kamaleddin Sodeyri
30.   Hazrat Darvish Mohammad Mozaheb Karandehi
31.   Hazrat Mir Mohammad Moemen Sodeyri Sabzevari
32.   Hazrat Mir Mohammad Taghi Shahi Sabzevari
33.   Hazrat Mir Mozafar Ali Shahi
34.   Hazrat Mir Mohammad Ali
35.   Hazrat Seyyed Shamseddin Mohammad
36.   Hazrat Seyyed Abdolvahab Naini
37.   Hazrat Haj Mohammad Hassan Kouzekanani
38.   Hazrat Agha Abdolghader Jahromi
39.   Hazrat Jalaleddin Ali Mir Abolfazl Angha
40.   Hazrat Mir Ghotbeddin Mohammad Angha
41.   Hazrat Shah Maghsoud Sadegh Angha
42.   Hazrat Salaheddin Ali Nader Shah Angha

The Oveyssi school of Sufism that dates from 7th century A. D., the advent of Islam, has at the present time 300,000 students and hundreds of centers throughout the world. New centers are continually forming, sometimes several in one city, to serve the different needs of pupils. The place and center of attendance for the purpose of receiving practical disciplines, and awareness is called "The Khaneghah" *House of God.*

The centers range from small study groups that meet for weekly classes to entire communities. They offer a variety of classes, gatherings, and seminars, which cover a wide range of different physical and metaphysical sciences from philosophy, literature, from poetry and learning how to read holy scriptures to telepathy, healing and magnetic therapy, spiritualism, science of Letters and Numbers and alchemy. Meditation classes are a crucial and important part of Oveyssi training and these practical classes are offered at each center.

Dr. Yoshimichi Maeda, a Japanese biologist who visited with the Spiritual teacher of the school in 1976, in the original center, at Sufi-Abad, in Karaj, 40 kilometers from Teheran, writes about the structure of the school of Sufism:

Its organizational structure is most interesting and unique: It is a highly professional group that operates like an independent society and sets a perfect example for those larger organizations that have been less successful in accomplishing such a solid infrastructure and self-sufficiency. Within the school are experts in design and construction as well as research groups in sciences, literature, and such fine arts as painting, sculpture and calligraphy.[4]

Today Sufism has changed in form if not in essence to deal with the modern world of science and stress. In the past and not very distant past at that, at the time of the 40th Pir of the Oveyssi school, Hazrat Mir Ghotbeddin Mohammad Angha, Sufism was an esoteric science and its instructions were not available to all. In earlier times, much mortification and self-discipline was endured by the few who attained this reality, for they had to prove they were worthy students first, before receiving any instruction from the Pir. However, beginning in 1950, the dwellings of Hazrat Shah Maghsoud Sadegh Angha, the 41st Pir of the school of Oveyssi, became open to all: he who deserved, he who did not, he who was a true seeker, he who was not. To all, the gates of the Khaneghah were opened and any newcomer was welcome to hear the secrets and the Truth. Especially today, Sufism, once dedicated to a very small and elite group, is being presented to the 20th century. The meetings and gatherings are no longer scarce but are frequent and open to all. Sufism, which has been centered for centuries where it was founded in Iran is no longer limited to the east, now the whole world can profit.

Knowledge is the priceless heritage of man. Sufism is the point where love and affection of the imperfect self meet that of the superior soul. This love will shelter and revitalize the entire world. It will draw man to God, the origin of love.

The famous Sufi poet, Mohy-al-din-Arabi, who received the grandeur of the Sufi life through divine inspiration, has written a book about his revelations titled "Fatouhat", meaning "victories". This victory is understanding the most complex areas of all science and philosophy. In our epoch, divine will has created a new plan for a stagnating world. Now, Sufism will bring life to this world of advanced science and technology. The banner of this triumph and spiritual conquest of the world is carried by the school of Islamic Sufism, MTO Shah Maghsoudi, under the direction and leadership of the present Pir of the school Hazrat Salaheddin Ali Nader Angha. The present headquarters of the school is located in San Rafael, Northern California.

As I mentioned earlier and contrary to general beliefs, Sufism is not self-mortification and resignation from daily life, rather it is the total knowledge of existence, including and covering all sciences. Physics is merely an inferior level of metaphysics, since it is metaphysics and the eternal law that have given birth to the physical world. Once we know the whole, the partial is also clear. Whereas, if we start studying the partial we shall not know the whole. As the famous Sufi poet Mahmoud Shabistari wrote in *The Garden of Secrets*, "The universe became man and man the universe." We shall explore this in the next chapter which is called, The Search for Truth Through Philosophy, Theology and Science.

CHAPTER TWENTY ENDNOTES

1.   Dr. Ronald Grisel, *Sufism*, Ross Books, 1983, P.O. Box 4340, Berkeley, Calif., 9470, p. 45.

2.   Jalaledin Rumi, *Massnavi Manavi*, Persian edition, 1925, Sepehr Publication, p. 716, line 1826.

3.   Ali Bin Uthman Al-Hujwiri, *Kashf Al-Mahjub*, Islamic Book Foundation 249-N Samanabad, p. 84.

4.   Shah Maghsoud Sadegh Angha, *Dawn*, Intro. by Dr. Yoshimichi Maeda, p. 2.

CHAPTER TWENTY-ONE

THE SEARCH FOR TRUTH
THROUGH
PHILOSOPHY, THEOLOGY AND SCIENCE

Imaginary philosophies do not provide positive and logical answers to the needs of the contemporary man.

Hazrat Shah Maghsoud Sadegh Angha

In this chapter I am going to consider the approach of philosophy, theology and science toward the search for Truth.

Philosophy

The root of the word "philosophy" comes from the Greek *philos* which means "love," and *sophia* which means "wisdom." The *Oxford Advanced Learning Dictionary* says, "Philosophy is the search for knowledge, the nature and meaning of things."

Theology

The root of the word "theology," is from the Greek *theos* meaning "God," and *logos* which means "discourse."

Theology according to *Encyclopedia International* is "the study of God, of man, and the world in relation to God."

The *Oxford Advanced Learning Dictionary* defines theology as "The formation of a series of theories about the nature of God and of the foundations of religious belief."

Science

According to the *Oxford Advanced Learner's Dictionary*, science is "knowledge obtained by observation and the testing of facts."

The *Random House Dictionary* defines science as systematic knowledge of the physical or material world gained through observation and experimentation.

Webster's Third New International Dictionary gives the following definitions for science.

- Knowledge obtained and tested through use of the scientific method; accumulated and accepted knowledge that has been systemized and formulated with reference to the discovery of general truths or the operation of general laws;

- Knowledge classified and made available in work, life, or the search of truth;

- Knowledge obtained and tested through use of scientific method. Such knowledge concerned with the physical world and its phenomena (natural sciences).

Philosophy, distinct from theology, began in Greece in the 5th century B.C. Philosophy, defined at that time as love and the pursuit of wisdom took all knowledge as its province. The quest for knowledge was born by man's instinctive curiosity about the world around him. The early philosophers undertook to describe and to explain the world around them, and also concerned themselves with matters of social and personal conduct, human values and principles, all of which had to be solved by contemplation and informal observation.

By the time of Plato (427-347) and Aristotle (384-322), philosophers were concerned with logic, mathematics, natural sciences, ethics, political theory, as well as aesthetics. As Christianity rose and Rome fell, philosophy was submerged by theology.

From the 11th to the 14th century, philosophy in the West was dominated by the Catholic Church. Philosophers continued to explain the nature of life until the 15th century when science started to unravel the mysteries and developed different methods of investigation. One result was a split from philosophy, and both became separate branches of learning.

Today, philosophy has become itself a "philosophical question." "There are no established methods, principles, or standards universally agreed upon by all philosophers. By and large however, it can be said that the essence of philosophy is systematic reflection upon experience to the end of obtaining a rational and comprehensive view of the universe and of man's place in it."[1]

In defining philosophy, theology, and science, Bertrand Russell, the 20th-Century philosopher claims,

> Philosophy is something intermediate between theology and science. Like theology, it consists of speculation of matters of which definite knowledge has, so far, been unascertainable; but like science, it appeals to human reason rather than authority. All definite knowledge belongs to science; all dogma, as to what surpasses definite knowledge, belongs to theology. But between theology and science there is a No Man's Land, exposed to attack from both sides; this No Man's Land is philosophy. Almost all the questions of most interest to speculative minds are such as science cannot answer, and the confident answers of the theologians no longer seem so convincing as they did in former centuries. The studying of these questions, if not the answering of them, is the business of philosophy.[2]

One wonders, "How?" It is not obvious yet? What are the means and tools that philosophy offers except human reason and speculation? Bertrand Russell answers, to our greatest surprise, by saying:

> "Philosophy aims at teaching us how to live with uncertainty and without being paralyzed by hesitation."[3]

Early philosophers would not agree. Philosophy started in the faith that beneath this apparent chaos there was a hidden permanence and unity. As a modern writer on philosophical methods has put it,

> There seems to be a deep rooted tendency in the human mind to seek ...something that persists through change.

Consequently the desire for explanation seems to be satisfied only by discovery that what appears to be new and different was there all the time. Hence the search for an underlying identity, a persistent stuff, a substance that is conserved in spite of qualitative changes and in terms of which these changes can be explained.[4]

The search has not been given up. Scientists are now looking for "a unifying force," a force that is the unification of all the fundamental forces (i.e., gravity, electromagnetic force, the weak force, and the strong force) of nature. "Experiments have now verified that the weak and the electromagnetic forces are really one and the same at high energies. We call this new unified force the electroweak force."[5]

In spite the different terminology, this search is not dissimilar to that of the early Milesians, the natural Greek philosophers of the 5th century, who were searching for a persistent and everlasting substance that would prove to be the basis of the world and all things in it. And today, "The eventual goal of science is to provide a single theory that describes the whole universe,"[6] says the 20th-century physicist Stephen W. Hawking.

The unified theory is what Einstein spent most of his later years searching for, although he was unsuccessful.

The discovery of a complete unified theory may not aid the survival of our species," says Hawking, "it may not even affect our lifestyle. But ever since the dawn of civilization, people have not been content to see events as unconnected and inexplicable. They have craved an understanding of the underlying order in the world. Today, we still yearn to know why we are here and where we came from. Humanity's deepest desire for knowledge is justification enough for our continuing quest. And our goal is nothing less than a complete description of the universe we live in.[7]

However, science has a much better chance at achieving this everlasting quest, since it uses a practical method of investigation as opposed to philosophy, which relies purely on human reason and intellect. The scientist is one who is free from any selfish motives or interest and thus analyzes by observation, aided by the experimental tools, measuring instruments, and other equipment needed to prove and produce facts. Science does not rely on theory alone and it claims nothing until it can offer objective evidence and verification.

Philosophy, on the other hand, is like an opinion or a state of mind that offers itself to be accepted or rejected, and promises no evidence or truth, and is not even reliable since it trusts its personal impressions and is capable of error.

Bertrand Russell notes that:

> Almost all the questions of most interest to speculative minds are such as science cannot answer: Is the world divided into mind and matter, and if so, what is mind and what is matter? Is mind subject to matter, or is it possessed of independent powers? Has the universe any unity or purpose? Is it evolving toward some goal? Are there really laws of nature, or do we believe in them only because of our innate love of order? Is man what he seems to the astronomer, a tiny lump of impure carbon and water or is he what he appears to Hamlet? To such questions no answers can be found in the laboratory. The studying of these questions, if not the answering of them, is the business of philosophy.[8]

"Imaginary philosophies," declares the Sufi Master, Hazrat Shah Maghsoud, "do not provide positive and logical answers to the needs of the contemporary man".[9]

Therefore, although many minds have endeavored to achieve the answers to the universal questions of life, use of speculation, imagination, and reasoning has been unsuccessful and there remain too many questions with no answers. Philosophers have presented theories of the universe, the human nature, the truth; each ended up explaining himself. Individual philosophies are somewhat like self-portraits; in trying to define the universe each philosopher describes himself. No more than this could be achieved by the help of the limited tool, the brain.

The philosophical and even the scientific approach to essential questions are based on theories that might be proven or disproven at any time. My goal is not to undermine the endeavors of science or philosophy, since any human being who wonders and questions his true nature and sees himself faced with fundamental questions and earnestly searches for the answers is worthy of much praise and respect. Yet even the scientific approach has its limitations in understanding our existence as the Absolute.

Hawking, one of greatest physicists of our time, points out that:

> Any physical theory is always provisional, in the sense that it is only a hypothesis: you can never prove it. No matter how

many times the results of experiments agree with some theory, you can never be sure that the next time the result will not contradict the theory. On the other hand, you can disprove a theory by finding even a single observation that disagrees with the predictions of the theory.

It turns out to be very difficult to describe the universe all in one go. Instead we break the problem into bits and invent a number of partial theories. Each of these partial theories describes and predicts a certain limited class of observations, neglecting the effects of other quantities or representing them by simple sets of numbers. It may be that this approach is completely wrong. If everything in the universe depends on everything else in a fundamental way, it might be impossible to get close to a full solution by investigating parts of the problem in isolation.[10]

However, the mind, being as limited as it is, does not have any other choice but to investigate the truth in this partial and limited way. Let us consider the mind and the process of thinking, based on scientific investigations, so that we will understand the mind's limitations.

What is thinking

The nature of thinking makes up a large part of the disciplines of philosophy, psychology, and education.

We will start by tracing the growth of thought from infancy when the mind is totally blank and follow its development to adolescence.

In infancy, thinking is associated with learning about the world and how to respond to it. At birth, the child is only limited to uncoordinated reflexes. These reflexes gradually coordinate with each other. The child looks in the direction of sounds, grasps what he sees, and brings before his eyes that which he grasps. The highest point of development, which signals the beginning of true thought, occurs when the child can perform "mental experiments." For example, the child brings an interesting object, such as a stick, within his reach; he has foreseen the entire action in his mind before actually grasping the object. He is manipulating objects with his mind first instead of with his hands.

Gradually, the world moves into the "mind" and consequently thought becomes less dependent on the world. This begins with the ability of the child to represent objects as images and thus give them permanence. Eventually, his thoughts become independent of direct perception and progress from the concrete to the abstract. This process increases as mental growth takes place.

Therefore, the earliest mental activities deal with images. More complex mental activities occur when the child can envision the use of a stick to reach for an object farther away. Significant progress appears when symbols replace mental images and thoughts are increasingly abstract.

Thought occurs as a result of chemical actions and reactions in the brain. Thinking is the mental manipulation of symbols, that is, a visual image, memory, feeling, thought, event, or representation of something in the mind. These are called sensual perceptions. The human tendency to solve problems is usually based on prior experience. The brain is very similar to a computer, it relies on and is limited to the data it receives or that it already has in storage. It cannot provide new information. Another problem is that its storage undergoes constant change. Upon receiving new information, a new addition or any change in its contents, new and different responses may develop, provisional responses are thus unreliable and subject to much change.

Like a computer that has to be kept at a moderate temperature to function and respond accurately, the mind can also be easily influenced by many factors. The mind does not always function at its best; a preoccupied mind, for example, can become confused and cluttered by numerous images. Even the best-working mind, however, is prone to constant change as it continually acquires new information and experiences.

> Sensual observation and experiences happen repeatedly. The mind is collecting information all the time. Not only is there a continual change in the brain storage, but the cells of the brain and the nervous system also change. Their renewal may be so slow as to fool us into believing that they may be eternal, or at least stable enough for a lifetime of recording and rearranging of memories.[11]

Can we be guided toward the discovery of that which is stable, the principles of existence and reality, by the power of this unstable and changeable tool, the mind? The answer is, "no." A computer is limited in the amount of information it receives and reacts accordingly. It will be unable to find a solution to a problem it has no information about. The mind acts and is limited in the same way.

Since the mind is limited, don't we need another source, one which is unlimited? And what is that unlimited source that can well lead us to the unlimited absolute knowledge, the truth? What is the measure with which we can measure the truth? Let us ponder this question while we read on.

The scientific approach for finding the truth is the collective efforts of scientists throughout history. The thrust of this collective effort is the hope of finding the truth at some unknown time in the future, but the problem with this is that every human being wants to know the truth of his own existence during his lifetime.

Theology, on the other hand, makes no possible endeavor to know anything and moves everything out of our reach; there must be a creator and therefore we must blindly believe him since he is God and the knower of all; everything remains as unsupported theory.

The philosopher tries to find a definition of the truth by reasoning, which is subject to individual interpretation and unreliable for leading us to the absolute truth.

If the scientist, the philosopher, or the theologian of our time cannot lead us towards the absolute truth, who has the answer? And what is TRUTH?

CHAPTER TWENTY-ONE ENDNOTES

1.   *Encyclopedia International.* Grolier Inc., New York, 1974, p. 286.

2.   Bertrand Russell, *A History of Western Philosophy*, Simon & Schuster, 1945, New York, New York, p. XIII of introduction.

3.   *Ibid.*, p. XIII of introduction.

4.   L. S. Stebbing, *A Modern Introduction to Logic*, (Methuen, 2nd ed. 1933), p. 404.

5.   Leon M. Lederman, and D. N. Schramm, *From Quarks to the Cosmos*, Scientific American Library, 1989, New York, N.Y., 10010, p. 127.

6.   Stephen W. Hawking, *A Brief History of Time*, Bantam, 1988, New York, N.Y., p. 10.

7.   *Ibid.*, p. 13.

8.   Bertrand Russell, *A History of Western Philosophy*, Simon & Schuster, 1945, New York, p. XIII of Introduction.

9.   Shah Maghsoud Sadegh Angha, *The Light of Salvation*, University Press of America, Lanham, MD, 20706, p. 79.

10   Hawking, *A Brief History of Time*, pp. 10-11.

11.   Shah Maghsoud Sadegh Angha, *Dawn*. University Press of America, Inc. Lanham, MD, 20706, p. 25.

CHAPTER TWENTY-TWO

SUFISM – THE REALITY OF RELIGION

The Sufi knows, while the philosopher wants to know.

Hazrat Slaheddin Ali Nader Angha

If the truth and absolute knowledge cannot be a product of our minds, despite imagination, reason or logic, and we want to go beyond the limited powers of the brain, then what do we do? How can we learn about the truth?

Let us address our question to the science of Sufism and hear what a Sufi believes, one who has discovered and knows the Truth.

> The "knowledge of reality, which is the true meaning of religion, is within the domain of practical Sufism, Erfan. The teachings of Sufism Erfan, encompass and transcend science and other theoretical and speculative learning."[1]

We must understand the "Knowledge of Reality" that Hazrat Shah Maghsoud refers to is not hard dogma and the blind acceptance of the Holy Scriptures represented by the theologians, nor is it knowledge one can acquire from books and by much learning. It is not knowledge acquired in the conventional way, but is Absolute Knowledge, acquired differently.

While the scientists hope to find the answers and the missing parts of the puzzle in the future, the Sufi is one who knows the Truth in his lifetime. This knowledge is not partial and it is not received through the senses or postponed to the far future, but is Absolute and is in the possession of the Sufi. Sufi is the one who knows the Truth and is the most knowledgeable one of his time and is defined *as the Man of his Time* by His Eminence Hazrat Ali.

The Sufi of our time, Hazrat Salaheddin Ali Nader Angha, in *The Wealth of Solouk* (about the stages of purification and awareness that the seeker of the Truth undergoes for the attainment of Absolute Cognition) says,

"The Sufi knows, while the philosopher wants to know."[2]

If, according to Sufism and the words of the Sufi Master, "that which is constant and unchangeable is the Truth," then we have to find a constant and unchangeable measure by which we can know the Truth. We cannot measure infinity with a yardstick, nor can we attempt to understand the mysteries of humanity with the changeable storage of the mind.

The prophet of Islam says,

"Knowledge is not in the heaven, to descend upon you, nor does it grow on earth, but it is with you."[3]

The Absolute Knowledge cannot be known through books, nor is this how the prophets instructed us. They themselves found the Truth through inner revelations, and then wrote them down as scriptures and holy books. But reading these revelations over and over again will not reveal the truth to us, for each must discover the truth for himself. How, one may ask? We can discover the truth the way the prophets did. Recall that Jesus Christ said, "You may be where I am," and Hazrat Mohammad also said, "I am a man, I hear the Angelic Voice."

The truth must be grasped intuitively through mystical experience rather than philosophical reflection and reasoning. It is an individual process; in the same way that we do not rely on others to eat and breathe for us, we have to experience religion and Truth for ourselves.

As a philosophy student I remember how fascinated I was when I first started to learn about the early Greek philosophers, but soon I became very confused. Which was true? I wondered. Among the different ideologies, which philosopher should I believe? The more I read and learned about different opinions and ideas the more confused I became. I needed a criterion with which to distinguish and choose the right philosophy from the wrong one. I was looking to find the truth of myself among all those different opinions. There were ones that appealed to me more than others. How could I trust my personal judgment? What was the measure of truth? And how could I really know?

When I became a student of Islamic Sufism, everything started to make sense and soon I found all my answers. I learned that it was not in my thoughts that I had to search for my answers, that my senses could not reveal the Truth to me; my mind was incapable of differentiating between right and wrong, truth or falsehood. My mind depended for its source of information on mere physical comparisons, action-reaction and other natural effects collected and gathered through the limited senses.

And even though the sciences provide solutions to the problems of physical life, they too are limited in their research and make no reference to spirituality in order to enhance their search for the discovery of Truth.

> The true scientists generally consider
> The past science merely as an introductory chapter;
> And reckon that the truly new spur
> Of knowledge springs from one's own true nature.
> The fountainhead of the knowledge's spring
> Is none but one's own essence, one's inner being.
> What scientists miraculously unearth through time
> Is barely a trifle introductory page
> To the book of supreme knowledge, the truth sublime,
> For the seeker venturing his inner self to envisage.[4]

CHAPTER TWENTY-TWO ENDNOTES

1.   Shah Maghsoud Sadegh Angha, *Dawn*, University Press of America, Inc. Lanham, MD 20706, p. 25.

2.   Salaheddin Nader Pir Oveyssi Angha, *The Wealth Solouk*, MTO Shah Maghsoudi Publication 1984, p. 26.

3.   Hazrat Mohammad, the prophet of Islam.

4.   Shah Maghsoud Sadegh Angha, *Manifestation of Thought*, University Press of America, 1988, p. 9.

CHAPTER TWENTY-THREE

THE MEASURE OF TRUTH IS TRUTH ITSELF

*That which is constant and
unchangeable is the Truth*

Hazrat Shah Maghsoud Sadegh Angha

In a world where everything is undergoing constant change, how can we find something stable? Everything seems so transient. The seasons constantly change the appearance of nature: Clouds move, water flows, leaves scatter, flowers wither. Feelings such as love and deeply rooted affection in our hearts can change so abruptly to feelings of hatred and even enmity. The physical body, young and beautiful – full of life and vigor – begins to age. Bountiful nature takes back its gifts, one by one; the senses dim, strength diminishes, organs fail, skin dries and cracks.

> Come, on the whim's palace don't depend.
> Serve wine, for life will soon end.

> I'm the slave of him, who under the blue sky,
> Is entirely free from all possessions, all ties.

> At the tavern last night when I was drunk and gay,
> I heard the angels good tidings say:

> 'O, ambitious falcon, don't fly so high,
> Your nest is the abode of sorrow and sigh.'

> From Heaven's turret was announced this call:
> 'This carnal snare doesn't fit you at all.'

> Remember my son! Never worry over sorrow,
> For passing troubles of today and tomorrow.

'Clear up your frowns, says the inner voice,
Be happy with your lot: there's no other choice.'

Don't seek much loyalty from Time and Tide;
For to many grooms this world-hag was the wedded bride.

There's no loyalty in the rose's smile.
O heartless nightingale! your cry lasts but a while.

Don't be envious of Hafiz's fluent verse,
It's a gift of the founder of the universe.[1]

Hafiz

Among all these apparent changes, however, according to Sufi discipline, lies a divine and everlasting being that is constant and unchangeable.

"That which is constant and unchangeable is the Truth," says the Sufi Master Hazrat Shah Maghsoud, who believes that which does not undergo change in two different times is genuine and immortal.

> In spite of many changes my genuine identity and stable innate being have not changed. I am the same person I used to be. I therefore have no reason to believe that this genuine identity did not exist before birth and will not continue to exist after death. Only that which does not change in two different times is genuine and immortal.[2]

The real identity is what each person calls the "I". This is the true identity that does not change, and because it does not change it is not subject to death; it is an unchangeable essence, stable and eternal.

Man consists of body and soul. "Soul is an incorporeal and non-material essence," says Vive Kananda, in his book *The Way of Cognition*, "and because it is not matter, it therefore does not follow the principles of cause and effect. So it is eternal and has neither beginning nor ending."

This true identity existed long before our body or our personality came into existence; it does not owe its existence to our physical body or anything physical. Quite simply, it is the presence of God within us.

> Therefore the cognition of religion is not step by step, but is the realization and the cognition of God and nothing else, which also means the cognition of 'I' that is constant and unchangeable. The 'I' is that divine inspiration of God's spirit breathed into Adam giving him life.[2]

The measure of the Truth can only be Truth itself.

All the natural characteristics of a seed; its adaptability, capability, its growth agents, and the perfect coordination of its living parts, are concentrated and preserved in that particular seed, all of which is based upon its essential and constant identity. If one paid careful attention to the trunk, branches, leaves, fruit of a tree, and could see the dominating force and power that guided the form and design and all the hidden characteristics of that beautiful tree, one could discover the genuine identity, in the seed itself. Of course, such observations do not belong to the level of physical and sensual discoveries.[3]

Sohrawardi, the famous Persian philosopher, says that man is in possession of a "Divine Seed." And Jesus Christ says, "The Kingdom of Heaven is like a mustard seed that man took and planted in his field. It is the smallest of all seeds, yet when it grows, it is the largest of garden plants and becomes a tree so that the birds of the air come and perch on its branches" (Matthew 13:31-32).

Like the apple seed, we too possess the potential of the "seed of knowledge" within us. We have therefore to live up to the finest element of our most noble nature; otherwise we have made no use of our inborn abilities and powers. Consequently our energy centers will become weakened and will not function as they were designed to, similar to a fruit tree that remains barren. Man therefore possesses great potential to love, to grow, and to create.

To look within is where the prophets have told us to look. It is the spring of knowledge. Every creative act and all creative thinking comes from this inner source of knowledge.

Stan Gryskiewicz, the director of innovation and creativity applications at the Center for Creative Leadership in Greensboro, North Carolina, says, "Creativity is a part of the human spirit, and it just keeps popping up." The works of great artists, musicians, writers and poets are but spiritual inspirations that come from within. The creativity that is right away apparent in their work so touches the depth of our being, as if its familiarity suggests that it might be from a part of us. It is that creativity which has long been the source of inner inspiration. This inspiration comes from another world, not the world of senses, and immediately the certain beauty strikes you as different and even angelic. It is that innate knowledge that has produced masterpieces of art and music, so sweet as to sound divine. These are not the products of the physical body and the physical brain, nor the outcome of chemical actions and reactions.

"Michelangelo claimed that he could see his figures locked inside their marble prison and all he did was to set them free by knocking away the extra pirces."[4] This is not a product of imagination but an inspiration that comes from a different source, the heart.

"The most beautiful thing we can experience," wrote Einstein, "is the mysterious. It is the source of all true art and science...to know that what is impenetrable to us really, manifesting itself as the highest wisdom, and the most radiant beauty that our dull faculties can comprehend only in their most primitive form. This knowledge, this feeling is at the center of religiousness."

The verses of the Koran are examples of the most beautiful and poetic literature; its rhythmic verses are so well organized that those who are familiar with Arabic place it in a totally different literary category. It's language is not understandable by just a native. Can these be anything but inner revelations inscribed upon the heart of Mohammad by the hands of the angel Gabriel. Was it not true that Mohammad the prophet of Islam could not read or write?

If the mind becomes pure and clear of all outer attractions and attachments of the physical plane, it can become inspired by the source of knowledge, the heart, and all intuition and knowledge will then be able to flow through it. It becomes as clear as a mirror on which the Truth of the heart will reflect and manifest its knowledge beyond the body, beyond the mental symbols and limitations. The computer or the mind will now receive programs and information from an unlimited source of knowledge, the heart, as opposed to the senses.

Only with the help of this criterion and measure of Truth, the I, the true identity within, is it possible to know the Truth, because it is the Truth. Sufism, or *Erfan* as explained by the Masters of Sufism, is the reality of religion and the cognition of the Truth. On the other hand, there is also philosophical *Erfan*, which is the theory of Sufism.

> Sufism is realized through the heart and the conscience; philosophy, on the contrary, is the result of mental processes. Thus, if Knowledge is based on the inward conscience, it is called practical Sufism. But if knowledge is a result of mental

activity, it is called philosophical Sufism. Sufism, in reality, cannot be defined. Whenever pure Sufism is converted into words and phrases, it should be known as philosophical Sufism.[5]

Religion in words and theory is meaningless and even absurd, and serves no purpose whatsoever. Again and again in the sermons of Hazrat Shah Maghsoud we repeatedly hear,

Words can not convey meaning, Nominal definitions are but veils that hide the Truth.[6]

Let us make this distinction between theory and practice even clearer by considering the following example: Imagine that someone you know wants to become a practical physician.. The student first has to study the theory of medicine during some eight years in medical school. Upon graduation, the student is not yet qualified to open a medical office; he must be able to pass an experimental period in a hospital to gain experience. During this trial period, the student tries to combine theory with practice. Only after this experimental period is the student able to practice medicine competently, putting in practical use what he has learned as theory, reaping the fruits of those long years of theoretical learning, and finally qualified to treat and cure the sick.

As much as the theory of Sufism is important, theory alone is worthless. Unfortunately, for many people, practicing religion today is too often a matter of repeating verbal prayers or going to church every Sunday or attending some ceremonies that take place a few times a year. Some are for mourning, especially in the Muslim tradition; others may be occasion for celebration, as is mostly true in the case of Christianity. It makes no difference if you mourn for the death of a particular Saint or prophet or if you celebrate his or her birth; it is no more than a tradition. We do not really know any saint or prophet, nor can we remember our cause for celebration once the event is passed.

Take Christmas for instance. It must have started as the celebration of the holy birth of Christ, as its name applies, a time of union with and remembrance of Christ. However, it has become a very costly period of the year when some people need to prepare for months in advance to fulfill the tradition of giving presents to friends and family. Perhaps the birth of Christ, the reason for Christmas, is the last thing on our minds as we dash through, in and out of shops in those last few hours, wondering if this shopping will ever be finished, absolutely preoccupied with finding suitable gifts and wondering about those we will receive!

In the case of mourning, which has become a strong tradition for unclear reasons in the Muslim tradition, it is the same situation. One might ask oneself, who am I mourning? Do I know him or her? In most cases, as in other religions, it is a cause of social gathering.

Obviously, the actual reasons for performing particular ceremonies have all but disappeared. They are repeated year after year, but if you ask someone, Why? What does this ceremony mean? What do you gain from it? they will say, "I don't know; we have always done so, ever since I remember."

I asked a Jewish friend once what he did for Hanukkah and what the ceremony stood for. He said he lit a candle every day for nine successive days. "How interesting," I asked, very curious to find out why. But he did not know why; he merely did so because his parents had done so, and he will undoubtedly pass this tradition along with many others to his family. And as times goes by, the reasons become even less important; what remains is the joy of giving and receiving presents and perhaps the holiday involved that allows one to rest or to travel. Or it can simply mean extra time to accomplish some unfinished work. But the cause of the celebration of Christmas is definitely not, in most cases, the birth of Christ or holy communion with him as the word *mass* implies.

"We are a very traditional family," said a Jewish woman quite proudly to me once. I was not familiar with this terminology. I had heard of being "religious" but not "traditional." When I thought about it I realized it was a different way of putting it, the same thing. Both are the same however, and are no more than performing certain acts at certain times of the year, repeating words and repeating meaningless actions with very limited understanding.

The Sufi of our time, Molana Salaheddin Ali Nader Angna, describes similar traditions and rituals in these terms: "It is like pretending to eat out of an empty plate; the food is missing." Where is the actual food? What do the Easter Bunny and chocolate eggs have to do with the resurrection of

Christ? No wonder people have turned away from this kind of religion. People can not find Truth in those ceremonies, the same way we cannot find food on an empty plate. This kind of religion does not attract the searching minds that are after the Truth. What is the point of repeating historical events over and over again? What does one achieve from doing so, a feeling that one is *religious*?! I doubt this can be religion. If this is religion then it seems like a dead religion with dead prophets and messengers. "You are wrong", says Jesus, "Because you know neither the scriptures nor the power of God. And as for the resurrection of the dead, have you not read what was said to you by God, 'I am the God of Abraham, and the God of Jacob'? He is not God of the dead, but of the living." And when the crowd heard it, they were astonished at his teaching.

(Matthew 22:29, 31-34)

In the Holy Koran we read:

Those who boasted that we killed Christ, Jesus the Son of Mary, The Messenger of God, they killed him not, nor crucified him, but so it appeared to them. And those who doubted him, they had no knowledge of him and did not follow but their thoughts and for surely they did not kill him.
Nay, God elevated him unto himself, God is exalted in power and wise.

(Surah 4:157 and 158)

This is the purpose of religion: Self-awareness, from the physical level to the most exalted stage, as introduced by Hazrat Mohammad, the prophet of Islam; "He whoever knows himself truly knows his God."[7] But this notion is completely forgotten and is perhaps the furthest thing from one's mind when attending religious ceremonies. Perhaps it is because we have no living prophets, no Savior, no Messiah, to show us the way to the Truth. We have killed and buried them all! The sad story of religion is, says Hazrat Shah Maghsoud Sadegh Angha, that "The Commandment of God still remains in the hands of the prophet."[8]

The difference between religion and theology is true knowledge gained through experience. Theology is a very good example of a description of food, on a menu. To have religion is to have that food. Is it wrong to talk about it? No. But talk of food is not food itself; it is crucial and vital to eat the food because only when you eat and drink do you stop being hungry and

CHAPTER TWENTY-THREE ENDNOTES

1.   Hafiz *Odes*, Translation from the Persian by Abbas Aryampur, Mazda Publishers, 1984, Lexington, USA., p. 36.

2.   Shah Maghsoud Sadegh Angha, *Hidden Angles of Life*, Multidisciplinary Publications, Pomona, Ca., 1975, p. 55.

3.   Shah Maghsoud, Sadegh Angha, *Dawn*, University Press of America, Inc. Lanham, MD, p. 26.

4.   Robert Coughlan, *The World of Michelangelo*, Time-Life Books, Inc. 1966, p. 96.

5.   Shah Maghsoud Sadegh Angha, *Dawn*, University Press of America Inc., Lanham, MD, p. 22.

6.   *Ibid.*, p. 21.

7.   Hazrat Mohammad, The prophet of Islam, *Holy Hadith*, MTO Publications, 1985, p. 70.

8.   Shah Maghsoud Sadegh Angha, *The Epic of Existence*, Persian edition, p. 117.

CHAPTER TWENTY-FOUR

SUFISM: THE THEORY OF UNITY

He whoever knows himself,
knows his God.

Hazrat Mohammad

"Existence, of which unity is the general law, is an entirety based on hierarchy," according to Shah Maghsoud Sadegh Angha.[1]

The doctrine of unity is the essence of Islamic Sufism. Unity, *tauhid*, is the general law. Physics and metaphysics are in union rather than total separation. Nature reflects the spiritual world; the supernatural reveals itself and gives of itself through nature, its graces running through the arteries of the universe like blood within the human body.

The Sufi seeks oneness with the Divine. Through the ecstasy of love, the barrier between God, *Allah*, and his creatures must gradually break down, resulting in this divine unity (*tauhid*). The Sufi finds his true self only when he loses his individual consciousness and through this oneness he is able to discover the Truth.

The Sufi poet Attar, in a richly allegorical poem called *The Conference of the Birds*, describes the mystical pilgrimage as a quest that begins with the stripping-off of all earthly desires, then continues with the progress through love, knowledge, and a sense of amazement, and ultimately to annihilation, which is uniting with God. In the *The Light of Salvation*, these seven stages are referred to by Hazrat Shah Maghsoud Pir Tarighat Oveyssi in the following poem.

> In the Kingdom of heart, seven stages there are:
> That the seeker of Truth must go, through them all.
>
> The first stage is to seek and yearn,
> With hardship and pain, he may earn.
>
> Faith is the heart's second stage,
> Its essence is eternal knowledge.
>
> The third stage is that of love,
> Mirror aglow with the light of love.
>
> One with existence the seeker becomes,
> In this stage, a witness of Truth he becomes.
>
> The fifth stage is that of UNITY,
> brilliant as the sun the particle will be.
>
> The sixth stage is that of ecstasy
> Full of Wonder the seeker will be.
>
> The seventh stage is annihilation and poverty,
> God will manifest in all to ye.
>
> In eternal peace thy heart shall live,
> When the seventh stage, thy home is reached.[2]

Islam introduces the unity and the last stage, where there is no longer a son and a father but where, the drop having reached the ocean, unity through love is attained. The soul, being divine in its essence, longs for union with that from which it is separated by the illusion of individuality and selfhood and to rise on the wings of ecstasy, the only means by which it can return to its original home.

Love is the alchemy of the human soul; it is that purifying fire that transmutes the alloy into pure and genuine gold. Love transcends the duality of reason and logic. Love is the force that unifies the whole existence. God is eternal love, as perceived by the Sufis. Hafiz says,

> The fire that never dies burns in our hearts,
> May the world never miss the plaint of lovers,
> The Exquisite Psalm, the breeze of joy.
>
> Odes, Hafiz

While the doctrines of Brahmanism are monistic based on the concept of "Oneness," Zoroaster proposes duality, God and the devil, and Christianity proposes a Trinity, the Father, the Son and the Holy Ghost. Islamic Sufism takes us to the "Original oneness" and unity. The individual drop reaches the ocean and becomes one with it, because it is of the same essence, water.

> To Allah belongs the kingdom of heavens and the earth. To Him all things return.

> (Koran 24:43)

When the wind ceases to blow, the waves merge with the ocean; similarly, when one's sense of duality, born of ignorance, is destroyed, one attains his original nature; the river merges with the ocean. Unity is experienced.

Religion has only one goal and *that is to know God*. In order to know God, one's true self must be found through ecstatic self-abandonment. The more a man knows God, the more he is lost in Him. "He whoever knows himself knows his God," says the prophet of Islam.

The following poem is a description of self-abandonment *(fana)* by Hazrat Salaheddin Ali:

> Hear from Salaheddin secretly,
> Annihilate thyself in love totally.

> Trapped within four dimensions,
> The body bound to boundaries and limitations.

> Sipping from the cup of desires, thou be,
> Never trying to overcome thyself willingly,

> In nature's wheels captured are thee,
> Though its ruler thou should be.

> If a devout and seeker thou be,
> In love you will find thy true identity,

> Life will open its arms to embrace thee,
> Humbly the sun will bow unto thee,

> Talk of I and we will no longer be,
> God thy only sovereign will be.

> Any polished heart will be,
> A mirror reflecting the Vali.

> Empty thy heart so may enter He,
> Of his wine, the cup filled be.[3]

As we have noted before, the heart is the holy place of revelation in Islamic Sufism. In much of Sufi poetry and prose, such writers as Rumi, Hafiz, and Attar, speak of the heart as the "winery," where "wine" refers not to a liquid but metaphorically to the essence of one's being. And the word "wine-bearer" *(saghi)* is often a reference to God, who symbolically pours wine into man's heart, and thus gives him life. The Holy Koran says,

> Your Creator will give you pure wine.

(Surah:76:21)

And Hafiz echoes the thought:

> Pour the wine from the Divine Cup
> Into the cup of your heart.
> Oh God, all other men are drunk with wine,
> Their drunkenness lasts but a single night,
> While mine abides forever.

Elsewhere, Hafiz seeks unity with the Friend – God:

> From the world's garden I desire one rose,
> Of all the greenery the shadow of the cypress, to repose.

> God forbid if the company of hypocrites I should join and admire,
> Of all good things of life, only the wine I desire.

> Paradise is promised for one's good deed,
> For us libertines, tavern will do indeed.

> Sit at the brook and watch the passing of time,
> T'is enough this sign of transiency of life.

> Watch the joys and the sorrows of the world.
> You may want it, but for me suffice this gain and loss.

> When the friend is with me nothing do I seek,
> His company makes me strong, though I am weak.

> O'Lord! to Hafiz paradise do not offer,
> Your Sanctuary to all existence I prefer.

Odes

CHAPTER TWENTY-FOUR ENDNOTES

1.   Shah Maghsoud Sadegh Angha, *The Manifestation of Thought*. p. 21.

2.   Shah Maghsoud Sadegh Angha, *The Light of Salvation*, p. 110.

3.   Salaheddin Ali Nader Angha, *Massnavi Ravayeh*, Publication United Press of America Inc., 1990, p. 3.

CHAPTER TWENTY-FIVE

THE LAW, THE WAY, THE TRUTH

Upon witness I declare that God is one
and that there is no God but God.

Hazrat Mohammad

In Chapter One, we explained there can be only one religion if we claim there is only one God. Of course, we have discussed how religion should not consist of mere traditional ceremonies and vague and unknown theories but should be based on true belief. This means that religion is experimental in the sense that it is only true for the one who has experienced it and found the truth by following the exact instruction of the prophets. The prophets came with the good news, that there is a God and each individual may know him.

Each prophet symbolizes a particular stage of this cognition. There is only one religion, although man had divided the one religion into many different religions and branches of the same religions. This one religion has three parts: 1) **The Law** *(shari'at)*; 2) **The Way** *(tarighat)*; and 3) **The Truth** *(hagighat)*.

No one part alone can lead one to the final stage, which is the Truth. The first stage, the Law, is Judaism. Moses received the Law, which was written on stone, and brought the Ten Commandments down from a mountain top to mankind.

Next came Christ who introduced the *Way*, the second stage. "Think not that I have come to abolish the Law and the prophets," he said.

> I have come not to abolish them but to fulfill them. For truly, I say to you, till heaven and earth pass away, not a dot will pass from the law until all is accomplished. Whoever then relaxes one of the least of these commandments and teaches men so, shall be called least in the kingdom of heaven.
>
> Matthew 5:17-21

Although we know Christ was a Jew himself, by the commandment of the Almighty he was appointed to extend the law to the next stage – The Way – and he was opposed and found guilty of blasphemy by the high Jewish priests and the elderly who could not accept that there could ever be anything but the Jewish religion.

Christ was crucified and the Law became empty ceremonial traditions that were handed down from generation to generation. The opening of the Truth, the freedom from captivity, the Holy promise, and the relationship with God did not flourish; it hardened into dogma and became a religion in itself called Judaism.

The Way, or the principles of the doctrine of Christianity, failed also to lead to truth but hardened to dogma, and the only thing that remains of Christianity today is, "Jesus died for us." Surely, the great mission of Christ was not to die, but to show the way to life, for he says, "I am the Way, I am the resurrection." The Way to the holy rebirth was the essence of his teachings.

The Way should have led to the final stage, the Truth. That final stage is called Islam, which means surrender *(tasl'im)*. Only in this total surrender to God can one reach the Truth and witness God. The Holy prophet of Islam, Mohammad, symbolizes the very last stage of religion. He brings the Message that God must be seen and witnessed, and that God must be known. His doctrine is one of unity. Islam, however, has undergone the same transformation as Judaism and Christianity. The practice in Islam today is not only empty ceremonies and meaningless messages but is far away from the Truth.

The Sufi revolts against this partial view of religions and the forms they have taken, largely a result of individual interpretations of those doctrines. The Sufi believes that there is a large distinction between asceticism *(zuhd)* and gnosis *(ma'rifat)*. One is blind faith and the other is true faith, acquired by personal experience, witness, and revelation, and as we have seen, this is exactly how the prophets discovered the Truth.

"There is no compulsion in religion," says the Koran 2:256. Hazrat Ali declares,

> I do not worship you my God in the hope of paradise, nor because of fear of hell, but I worship you because indeed you are worthy of praise and worship.

The mystical life, whose purpose is the pursuit of the Absolute Knowledge and the Truth, is not only compatible with observance of the Law *(shari'at),* but includes it as a facet or an aspect of a whole. The next stage is the way that leads to the Truth.

For those entering this mystical path, a spiritual guide *(pir)* is indispensable. He is called the "Mashiach" by the Jewish or "Messiah" by the Christians, and "Mehdi," by the Muslims. He is the Savior that everyone is waiting for. He is, however, always present for the souls who need guidance and he presents himself to them. Such a spiritual guide is not self-trained but is instructed and appointed by God himself. The savior is one who knows the Way *(tarighat)*. This path should be the one that leads to God and that God has appointed, not a path that suits individual interests and likings.

There are different stages *(maghamat)* the seeker of Truth *(salek)* goes through with the help of the Savior, *Pir Tarighat*. It is called the holy pilgrimage. The first stage is repentance *(tauba)*, which means turning toward God. The voyage continues until the experience of oneness with God is reached. This final stage is the last stage of religion: Islam, the total surrender, the lover finally uniting with the beloved.

In Sufism, the Law *(shari'at)* is considered "the boat," which symbolizes the means; it remains on land until it is set on its way, the water. The water symbolizes the Way *(tarighat)*. But of what use is a boat and the ocean if you do not have a destination to reach and a purpose to fulfill? The final stage of religion, the total surrender, is reaching the plane of Truth and acquiring the pearl from the depth of the ocean. That pearl is the real Truth.

Hafiz warns seekers about the dangers of the ocean, its storms, and dark nights, all of which symbolize the difficulty of the Way that leads to the Truth:

> The sea-dive seems easy with the hope of gain;
> But the pearl is it worth the storm and pain!
>
> Those secure on the shore with peace of mind,
> Don't know our storm, the waves, and the dark night!

Odes

Islam represents total surrender and witness and finally unity with the one witnessed.

> Hafiz this life is given to you by the Friend,
> Surrender – when you meet Him – in the end.

Odes

Without witnessing the Truth, cognition is not complete. The chemical actions and reactions of the brain can not reveal the Truth to us. *"Ashado-An- la -elaha-el- Allah;* upon witness I declare that God is one and that there is no God but God," says Hazrat Mohammad the prophet of Islam.

> The heart in no way falsified
> That which it saw.

(Koran 53:11)

CHAPTER TWENTY-SIX

ZEKR
SUFI PRACTICE

*Zekr is the reality of the seeker's journey from
the outer world to the world within.*

Hazrat Shah Maghsoud Sadagh Angha

Zekr, incorrectly translated as "*chanting*," is not the repetition of a word such as a *mantra*, but the remembrance of God.

In Islamic Sufism, calling the name of God joins the body, the tongue, the heart, and the mind in perfect harmony to make one statement, "There is no God but Allah" *(la-elaha-el-Allah)*. This is an affirmation that involves the *zaker's* (the one saying the zekr) whole being. By continuous remembrance and the utterance of Allah, the name of the beloved, one loses oneself in Allah.

"Zekr," according to Hazrat Shah Maghsoud, "is the constancy of the Light of Knowledge in the presence of the Heart and in the discovery of Truth in the hidden realms. It is the reality of the seeker's journey from the outer world to the world within."[1]

In contrast to the chanting performed in Transcendental Meditation (which was concerned with the effect of the rhythm of the mantra on the body), the Sufi zekr, *remembrance* of God, takes one the farthest away from the body, in fact, from everything but God. As we have discussed, verbal repetition of a word, even if it is the name of God, cannot bring about awareness, knowledge, and union with God. Zekr has to take place in the heart; zekr is true communion with God. For example, when one is in love one proves it not only verbally by saying *"I love you"* over and over again but also in actions, feelings, and expressions of affection.

However, we borrow and take what we like from religion and because we do not know what religion is, right away we discard it. We are therefore left with an action that has no meaning because we are just imitating an act outwardly. "I was given a special word to repeat," said one of my students who had attended chanting classes. You may chant and repeat a word, but that is not zekr.

The zekr that, according to the prophet of Islam, must save you, is "Say there is no God but Allah (God), and you will be saved" or *Ghulu la-elaha-el-Allah toflehou.* In order to experience the "oneness" of God, one's whole being must join to make that statement of unity for there is only to be God and nothing but God. As long as there is me and God, there is duality and Islam introduces unity. Then there is no discord, the mind and heart join, the body follows the unified action in a beautiful motion; all is a state of harmony.

The numerous verses in the Koran that condemn hypocrites *(monafegh)* refer to the disharmony that exists in religious performances. This makes a prayer only verbal and without true harmony and heartfelt belief.

Omar Khayyam tells a story of a religious man, a Sheikh, who lived next door to a prostitute.

> A pretentious Sheikh, to a prostitute called out,
>
> "Woman, You are drunk," he criticized!
> "And in the act of sin caught up!"
> "Yes!" she replied, "whatever you say, I am!
> But are you truly who you say you are?!"

The religion of a Sufi involves his whole being and it is not pretentious. He who wants everybody to think he is pious has no relationship with God.

"Beware of practicing your piety before men in order to be seen by them," says Jesus Christ, "for then you will have no reward from your Father in Heaven" (Matthew 6:1).

"When you pray, you must not be like hypocrites; for they love to stand and pray in the synagogues and at the street corners, that they may be seen by men. But when you pray, go into your room and shut the door and pray to your Father who is in secret; and your Father who sees in secret will reward you" (Matthew 6:5-6).

"And when you fast do not look dismal, like hypocrites, for they disfigure their faces that their fasting may be seen by men. But when you fast, anoint your head and wash your face, that your fasting may not be seen by men but your Father who is in secret; and your Father who sees in secret will reward you" (Matthew 7:17).

The religious acts of a Sufi are real and true because they aim at the capture of the pearl from the depth of the sea. Not only are these acts not pretentious but they are the only reward the Sufi aims for: the union with the beloved upon witnessing Him within.

In the Holy tradition Hazrat Ali asked, "Prophet of Allah, guide me through the shortest and the quickest way to God, and the easiest way for the servants of God, and the way of the chosen of God." The Prophet of Allah said, "Ali, it is in the constant and solitary zekr of God." Then he asked; "Prophet of Allah, show me then the way of Zekr." Then the Prophet said, "Close your eyes and Listen. Then three times he said *la-elaha-el-Allah* and Hazrat Ali heard and said three times; he listened and heard."[2]

This is not mere repetition of words but an experience of true union. Yet from the point of view of someone who might be unfamiliar with zekr, it may just seem to be an outward action and simple repetition only. In fact when zekr becomes a performance of this kind, it is not real and will not lead to the union, which is goal of zekr.

The "Sufi dance" has also become an outward performance of some renown. New students frequently ask me if I have Sufi dances in my classes. There are even classes that teach the Sufi dance! Sufi dance is not like the Iranian folk dance or the Arabian belly dance or rock and roll dances. It is a spiritual state.

The first Sufi who danced was in blissful communion with his beloved God. Upon witnessing and grasping the Truth within, he began dancing, his heart overflowing with joy and love. To one observing, it was a dance, but to the Sufi it was the expression of a true revelation from within.

> Last night at dawn I was relieved of grief,
> the water of life I was granted in brief.
>
> In ecstasy God's Manifestation I could see,
> The transformation cup was given to me.
>
> What a blessed sight, what a glorious night!
> A unique experience and a wonderous sight.
>
> In mirror of God's beauty my face did shine,
> To me were unfolded many secrets divine.
>
> No wonder that in spirit I feel sublime,
> For I needed blessings – they came in time.
>
> "Good news! Great fortune," a mysterious voice said.
> Upon hearing the good news I could withstand all the pain.
>
> All the honey that drips from my tongue,
> Is my reward for suffering so long.[5]

Odes of Hafiz

It is the absolute ecstasy within that makes the Sufi move involuntarily, and that seems like a dance, and not vice versa. We cannot imitate a Sufi by trying to dance as he dances. In order to really experience the Sufi dance, one has to first become a Sufi and dance as one discovers the Truth and not every Sufi dances!

Salat

The word *salat*, meaning prayer, literally means "call." The true call must be with the acceptance of God, which means that it must be at His will. The true and complete prayer is to call and to desire God, and to recognize one's own self and desires as inconsequential in the presence of the Lord, and one's self as ephemeral and God as eternal. This is the meaning of true prayer; hence man's own will has no part in the reality of prayer.

A God who is worshipped for the sake of worldly fulfillment is not great. For this reason any intention other than seeking closeness to God nullifies the meaning of prayer. Sheikh Safieddin Ardebili has said, "Zekr is the most important element in *salat*." The Zekr of God brings inner purification and prevents the heart from transgression. Ali-ibn-Tostari has said, "Zekr is leaving the sphere of neglect to the realm of cognition in awe and intensity."

Salat is the most important practice of Islam and is considered the pillar of religion. The inner reality of prayer, however, consists of mysteries that are confirmed in the works of the Sufis."[4]

Meditation is the means to true *salat* prayer. Without meditation the prayer will be verbal and physical; its aim is not true communion and oneness with God.

CHAPTER TWENTY-SIX ENDNOTES

1. Sadegh Angha, *The Light of Salvation*, p. 96.

2. *Ibid.*, *The Light of Salvation*, p. 101.

3. Shirazi Hafiz, *Odes*, Mazda Publication, Lexington, KY, 1984, p. 132.

4. Sadegh Angha, *Al-Salat*, pp. 31-2.

CHAPTER TWENTY-SEVEN

MEDITATION: PRACTICAL SUFISM

Of what is significant in one's own existence one is hardly aware, and it certainly should not bother the other fellow. What does a fish know about the water in which he swims all his life?

Albert Einstein

Meditation is practical Sufism. In Chapter Twenty-three, we discussed the theory of unity. Meditation is its practice and experience. As May Mohs once said in a 1987 issue of *Discover Magazine*, "Roses don't smell as sweet as they used to – where has all the fragrance gone?" Meditation is the practice of religion with its reality and fragrance intact, in contrast to a religion whose words and theory are like a rose without fragrance.

By now we have realized that absolutely nothing can be revealed and transferred through words. Every verse and word of the sacred and holy texts hide the true meaning and are no more than symbols for hidden treasures. Meanings can only be revealed by God – these meanings flash upon the inward eye in moments of meditation.

They know not, nor do they discern; for the Lord has shut their eyes, so that they cannot see, and their minds, so that they cannot understand.

(Isaiah 44:18)

> But even yet the Lord hasn't given you
> hearts that understand,
> or eyes that see
> or ears that hear.
>
> (Deuteronomy 29:4)

> For the Lord has poured out upon you
> a spirit of deep sleep.
>
> (Isaiah 19:10)

> Bring forth, the people who are blind, yet have eyes,
> Who are deaf, yet have ears!
>
> (Isaiah 43:8)

> The Lord sets the prisoners free;
> The Lord opens the eyes of the blind.
> The Lord lifts up those who are bowed down.
>
> (Psalms 146:8)

In the New Testament we also read:

> Why do you not understand what I say?
> Is it because you cannot bear to hear my word?
>
> (John 8:43)

> He who is of God hears the words of God;
> The reason why you do not hear them
> is that you are not of God.
>
> (John 8:47)

> But blessed are your eyes,
> For they see, and your ears, for they hear.
> Many a Prophet and godly man has longed
> to see what you have seen,
> And to hear what you have heard but could not.
>
> (Matthew 13:14-17)

The Koran also makes mention of the fact that if hearts were unsealed, the Truth would be manifested.

> And we have put coverings over their hearts,
> Lest they should understand the Koran,
> And deafness to their ears.
>
> (Surah:17 Verse:46)

> God hath set a seal on their hearts,
> And upon their hearing, and on their eyes, is a veil.
>
> (Surah:2 Verse:7)

It is for this reason that the MTO school of Islamic Sufism rejects any interpretations of the Koran, interpretations mean an endless variety of divergent and even contradictory beliefs. During the history of Islam and even today we see such false interpretations made by fanatics. These people can be divided into two groups: The first are the people who want to use religion for other means, such as politics, and for the exploitation of others. The second group are those who are ignorant about their religion and are thereby misled and exploited by the first group. So, ignorance, greed, and fanaticism are represented as Islam in most places today. And the result is poverty, ignorance, misery, and darkness, whereas Islam is the religion of knowledge, light, love, and unity. The true goal of religion is to unite with God through a most passionate love, like a spiritual love affair.

> My life candle is by God's love aglow,
> My whole life at God's threshold I throw.

> In memory of friend's eyes, myself destroy,
> Thus fulfill my old convenant to my joy.

> O! Zephyr, my bleeding heart, like the rose,
> To friend's fragrance as ransom I expose.

> Hafiz, hatred and sham remove, the peace of heart,
> The libertine – love I choose to be my part.[1]

In the *Sufi path of love*, the spiritual teachings of Rumi, the Persian Sufi, constantly refers to two kinds of knowledge and vision, which, according to the teachings of the prophet Hazrat Mohammad, he classifies into two categories: "One that discerns only form, and another that passes beyond form and discerns the meaning." The first he sometimes calls the "Science of bodies" *(Ilm-il abdan)* to distinguish it from the "Science of religion" *(Ilm-il adyan)*. The former embraces all that we customarily understand by the term "science" and "knowledge," including such disciplines as theology and metaphysics, for these are learned by study. Until they rise from the heart as the result of a direct vision of the inward meaning, or of God himself, they are but shadows, not light. Without a direct and vibrantly living vision of meaning, knowledge is only form. Certainly it may have the potential of being transmuted into true knowledge, but only after a long spiritual journey. Rumi says: "A knowledge is needed whose root is upon the other side, since every branch leads to its roots." "The painting on the wall is the likeness of a man," says Rumi, "look at the form. What does it lack?"[2]

The holy scriptures are understood not by those who read or speak Arabic but only by the Sufi who has experienced the meaning in his heart and therefore knows. As the Prophet of Islam says:

> Knowledge is not acquired through much learning, but it is the
> light shone upon the heart by the Lord. Thus, the heart of
> whom He will is illuminated by the Light of Wisdom.

This understanding derives from a supreme experience as a super-
intellectual, God-given knowledge, and belongs only to those who see God
with their hearts. The meaning of the Koran is infinite and reveals to each
genuine seeker *salek* in proportion to the spiritual capacity with which he is
endowed.

The Koran is made up of 114 Surah, the knowledge of which each
individual has in himself, since he also has a book made up of 114 Surah
within his heart. This knowledge is available, by God's grace, as one starts to
read his own book. Hazrat Shah Maghsoud says,

> Away from one's reality if one stayed
> An unopened Book he remained![3]

"Sufism, *Erfan*, is not a new religion, nor a denomination. It is the
reality of religion the way through which each Prophet discovers his most
exalted spiritual state and human values."[4]

The Sufi is one who worships God for the sake of God alone because
he has witnessed God and knows Him. He worships Him because he loves
Him. He does not worship an image or an idea, or a phantom in his mind.
He is one who watches over his heart. When his thoughts are collected and
every care is dismissed he is ready for communion with God, his heart he
guards from all else.

Sufi meditation is not the aimless wondering and drifting of the mind
into a void, or emptiness, but on the contrary it has a definite goal and is a
means of a holy communion with the God that lives within, and to witness
Him.

Each life is a cycle, but one that turns within the millions of other
orbits to which it belongs. A single proton is related not only to its own
nucleus but to all other atoms nearby in its neighborhood, and to the
molecule they form, and by their behavior toward every other atom in the
universe. In the same way there is a relationship between man and all of
existence. Mankind yearns toward the truth as plants turn to the sun.

"Of what is significant in one's own existence one is hardly aware, and it certainly should not bother the other fellow. What does a fish know about the water in which he swims all his life?"[5] says Albert Einstein.

Meditation helps each individual to harmonize with all existence and to find the ultimate Wisdom, the reason for one's being. Meditation is the link with the Divine.

Meditation is not mere concentrated thought, but a spectrum of human potential. The goal of meditation is hightened experience, perfected awareness, growth, and inner evolution, in order to be able to function according to one's full potential.

"Fragmented natural energies go to waste, and result in the loss of sensual subtilty, like a machine whose parts work individually and separately, it too becomes unusable,"[6] according to Hazrat Shah Maghsoud. Meditation helps us gather our scattered energies into a healthy whole.

Meditation is an exact science. It is an experimental study of inner processes, a method comparable to modern sciences, which studies primarily external events.

"The immaterial can only be discovered through the source of Life in the heart and traveling through the Kingdom of Heaven. This is what the prophets' teachings are based on. The centrality of the brain has been known as an intruder on the spiritual orders and the solitude of the heart."[7]

In the message of the soul, the Sufi Master claims that if the brain comes under the influence of the heart and functions in harmony with the heart, then it too would function from the limitless source of intelligence, instead of from the usual mental sources that are dependant on the changeable and unstable storage and data processing of the brain.

> Enlighten the channel that extends from your heart to your brain and do not allow the heart and the brain to live apart, like two unfriendly neighbors unaware of each other.[8]

When we practice meditation, the mind goes deeper and deeper within, and becomes more quiet. When it becomes free of thoughts the mind is able to touch its own source, becoming a mirror to the light and knowledge within. The Holy Koran confirms:

> Lo! therein verity is a reminder
> For him who hath a heart,

or giveth ear,
With full intelligence,
And he is witness.

(Surah: 50 Verse: 37)

"Guidance," explains the Sufi Master Hazrat Shah Maghsoud, comes through the union of thoughts, senses, nature, and the heart; going astray is disarray and confusion among these four elements. To become eternal, dissipate any desire that tends to grow in your heart through the union of the heart and brain. When all the combined energies reach the heart and have no tendency to leave, you will find yourself. And because you will be nourished from the source of life in your heart, you will see your enlightened soul. *Every bird flies back to its nest at nightfall and there finds comfort. So you, too, gather all the strength that is spread in your senses and body, in your heart at night and manifest your luminous figure.* If you receive life from the source of life in your heart, you will no longer be subject to death.

For a man continuously creates illusions that are shattered later; he creates these illusions but is not created by them. The essence of the existence is eternal, however, and will not vanish. Only the unstable will constantly gather and fall apart, while nothing is added or taken away from existence. The source of life is the creating angel of God; hence the birth of things is not for the purpose of increasing or decreasing the existence. This infinite diffusion, from the partial to the whole, from the atom to the universe, brings forth constant births that sink into dispersion and gathering, and yet the truth and the essence of life are eternal and immortal.

There are 101 channels, starting from the source of life in the heart, that, through 71,000 lines irrigate the 10 billion brain cells, so that the creation of God in this diffusion and gathering is brought to perfection. The source of life resides on the border between the heavens and the earth, and serves the will of God. At the point where the consciousness of life and the sleep of death confront each other, the first longs for eternity and the latter is attracted toward transience.

Search for Truth in your heavenly double, in the heart, the point of union of the two worlds, one delicate and one harsh, between sleep and wakefulness. The source of life in the heart is the light of knowledge and certainty and the very knowledge itself.[9]

In reality there is no distinction and separation between nature and divine, or physics and metaphysics or, as defined by Plato, the visible and the intelligible, but we in our shortcomings, separate these things. The reality is one, only we need to acquire full vision.

All great teachers urge us to realize the "divine" in this life through purity, self-control, and the recognition of "His presence" within us. This is the purpose of meditation.

Religion is the fulfillment of life; it is an experience in which every aspect of being is raised to its highest state. What is needed to attain this, however, is not dogma, but rebirth, an inner revolution.

> Except a man be born again he cannot see the Kingdom of God.
>
> (John 3:3)

This rebirth can take place only through higher knowledge and meditation, not through external acts, living habits, or vocal prayers alone. Meditation is the greatest and the most elevated experience of love.

> That which imagination never conceived,
> Reason and understanding never perceived,
> Has entered my soul from you.
> Therefore to you alone I turn to worship.
> Jalal-al-din Rumi

CHAPTER TWENTY-SEVEN ENDNOTES

1.   Hafiz, *Odes*, p. 86.

2.   Chittick, pp. 25, & 27.

3.   Shah Maghsoud Sadegh Angha. *The Epic of Existence*, Behjat Publication, 1974, p. 95.

4.   Salaheddin Nader Angha, *Peace*, p. 59.

5   Albert Einstein, *Out of My Later Years*, Bonanza Books, New York 1990, p. 5.

6.   Shah Maghsoud Sadegh Angha, *The Manifestation of Thought*, p. 14.

7.   Shah Maghsoud Sadegh Angha, *The Hidden Angles of Life*, p. 74.

8.   Shah Maghsoud Sadegh Angha, *The Message from the Soul*, p. 41.

9.   *Ibid.*, p. 42.

CHAPTER TWENTY-EIGHT

SPIRITUAL GUIDE

Each man, through personal experience and inward discovery, is able to cognize and establish the Truth of his own being.

Hazrat Slaheddin Ali Nadder Angha

Around the 5th century B.C., while the philosophers were pondering the mysteries of life, trying desperately to find the truth, the wise and knowledgeable Socrates appeared and left his mark on history and humanity.

By the second half of the 5th century, philosophers had begun to show interest in studying human life. Greece was a democracy, and Athens, the center of great thinkers, allowed most citizens to participate in their city's affairs. It became necessary for men to understand the nature of the real world in which they lived and the everyday problems they had to deal with. This was also reaction against the physical speculation of the philosophers, "a revolt of common sense against the remoteness and incomprehensibility of the world as the physicists presented it," says Guthrie, in *The Greek Philosophers*. Therefore, purpose of human life and its religious and political aspects became of concern. This reaction towards humanism is associated with the rise of a new class, the Sophists.

The Sophists were not a particular philosophical school, but rather a profession. They were itinerant teachers who made a living out of the new hunger for guidance in practical affairs. Although the word *sophistes* stands for "practitioner of wisdom," they are best known for their skepticism for they denied any possibility of absolute knowledge.

Socrates, in complete disagreement with the Sophists, contributed a lifetime of struggle and reaction against skepticism and the shifting of philosophical interest to human virtue and man's excellence. Realizing one's ignorance as the first stage toward knowledge was perhaps one of Socrates' most meaningful doctrines. "Know thyself" is also attributed to Socrates, for he believed that knowledge is attainable, but only after one has become totally aware of one's ignorance, for as long as he thinks he knows he will never learn.

There have always existed great sages who, like Socrates have been guided by God's power to explore their own true nature and to discover the mysteries of life and the universe. After the acquisition of inner knowledge through divine revelation, the great sages taught what they had discovered to those eager disciples who came to them.

"By God's grace he who searches findeth," says Hazrat Mir Ghotbeddin Mohammad Angha Pir Oveyssi. In his book *From Fetus to Paradise*, he wrote,

> The subtle path, although very close, seems far and is impossible to traverse alone. Supposing one does traverse the path alone, without the help of a special guide of path, that which he acquires are still heavenly gifts form the distinguished. But, because he has not taken the main route, he is immature and incomplete among his peers. A flower not raised by the hands of a wise and experienced gardener, is wild and self-grown, even though it may rise up from the sun.[1]

The Italian poet Dante says, in his book, *Canto*,

> To all, the Primal Light sends down Its ray
> Throughout all the universe God's ray
> Enters all things according to their merit,
> And nothing has the power to block its way.

The commandments of saints and prophets are the carriers of inspiration and revelation, and although they are meant for every man, only the harmonious and uniform have accepted them, while to the majority their sweet and meaningful messages have seemed bitter! Therefore, let the eager seekers hear the aid and guidance of a spiritual teacher. Without such direction and wisdom, one's individuality will never be rooted out and without such knowledge of light, the darkness of one's ignorance can never be destroyed.

Darkness is nothing new; it is familiar and ancient. Equally ancient is our search for light and knowledge. In this journey toward light, some have been wandering from temple to temple, mosque to mosque, ashram to ashram, church to church, and course to course. How does a person who walks in darkness know where to go; how can he look for light when he has never seen it? Shouldn't one seek the help of one who knows the light, who has experienced it? And then, what is the significance of the teacher and how can we find the right one out of so many existing ones?

A spiritual teacher is not a personal choice, like a piano teacher, but appointed by God. In spirit he is the Messenger of Truth, the one who was once called Buddha, Moses, Jesus Christ, Hazrat Mohammad. They are one in essence; the only difference is the outer appearance. They are but one light emanating through different lamps.

> We have sent on to you a messenger, from you,
> Who will read to you, our revelations,
> And will purify you of sin,
> Who will instruct you 'The Book,' and Wisdom,
> And teach you that which you have no knowledge.
>
> (Surah 2: Verse 151)

And in the Bible, we read:

> Behold, I send my messenger before thy face,
> Who shall prepare thy way;
> Prepare the way of the Lord,
> Make his paths straight.
>
> (Mark 1:2)

The Messengers of God brought the Message of Truth to man as they had received it. The Message of Truth is like a seed of knowledge. Therefore the Messengers symbolize the cultivation of this seed.

"The kingdom of Heaven," says Jesus Christ, "may be compared to a man who sowed good seed in his field" (Matthew 13:24). However, in order for a seed to grow a gardener is necessary, who needs to be present to help the seed grow into a full-grown plant – and bear fruit. This is a teacher who needs to be present at all times; he is the one who is within each seed. He is

Ali, or, as Jesus Christ calls him, "Eli." The Muslims call Ali, *Hojat-Allah.* *Hojat,* means mirror and Ali is the mirror that reflects God. On the cross, "Jesus cried with a loud voice, Eli, Eli, My God, my God, why hast thou forsaken me?" (Matthew 27:46).

Hazrat, which is placed before the name of the prophets, as in *Hazrat Mossa* (Moses), *Hazrat Eyssa* (Jesus), *Hazrat Mohammad, Hazrat Ali,* comes from *Hazer,* which means "to be present." The Messenger of God is not dead; the spirit is alive and eternal. He is always present within each heart. The Muslims can stop mourning! "Do not weep for me but weep for yourselves," says Jesus Christ, before his crucifixion. Weep for your children. For behold, the days are coming when they will say, "Blessed are the barren, and the wombs that never bore, and breasts that never gave suck! Then they will say to the mountains, 'Fall on us' and to the hills 'Cover us'" (Luke 23:29-31).

This spiritual guide and teacher must be revealed unto each soul. To the true seeker, the spiritual guide and Messenger is revealed within in the utmost secret sanctuary of his soul. When he is seen and witnessed within, then there remains no doubt.

> "God hath set a seal on their hearts,
> And upon their hearing, and on their eyes, is a veil."
> (Surah 127, Verse 7)

Upon the removal of the veil that is drawn over the hearts, the truth is manifested. Only the veils have to go away. Only by God's will is this possible.

Going back to Oveyss Gharani, we recall that he had never actually visited and met with the prophet, but was guided and instructed by him and knew him even better than those who had lived with him.

This Messenger within is the one that the Buddhists, Jews, Christians, and the Muslims are waiting for! They call him by different names: He is Maitreya, the Masiach, or the Messiah, or the Imam Mehdi. For those whose hearts are blind, the Savior will never come. The Savior that must save their soul must be witnessed and found within. The Savior is always present and has come for the souls that long for liberation. It is not in nature that we should look for him. For we shall only recognize him when we have seen and witnessed him within. Otherwise, we cannot know him, and if we make a choice of teacher in nature, it will be our choice, but it will not be the one who is appointed by God, who must teach us Wisdom and read our Book to us.

This is the way of Truth and true liberation according to Islamic Sufism; the guidance is from within. Thus the essence of the Sufi's message is that "each man, through personal experience and inward discovery, is able to cognize and establish the Truth of his own being,"[2] according to Hazrat Salaheddin Ali Nader Angha, the present teacher and the forty-second teacher of the school of Sufism.

> Splendid happy bird that has found a dwelling in love!
> How should any but the 'Angha'
> find place and lodging in 'Mount Ghaf'?
> Love, whose trade is joy, sweet speech and sweet thought,
> snatch now the veil from the face of that veiled King.
> Wherever you go, you are with me still,
> You who are my sight,
> transport me to annihilation if you will
> O, Lovers, Lovers, the time of union and encounter has come!
> You who came with torch and at dawn ravished my heart,
> dispatch my soul after my heart,
> do not seize my heart alone.
> Do not in rage and envy make my soul a stranger to my heart,
> Do not leave the former here,
> and do not summon the latter alone.
> Send a royal Message, issue a general invitation,
> How long, O Sultan, shall the one be with you
> and the other alone?
> You are my soul, and without my soul
> I know not how to live.
> You are my eyes, and without you, I cannot see!
> Prostrating myself, I said;
> 'Convey this prostration to that sun who by his burning glow,
> converts hard rock to gold.
> After all, how long will you keep in exile this vagrant heart?
> My body is like the moon, melting away out of love,
> My heart is lie Venus' harp may its strings be snapped!
> Watch the moon melting, Venus' broken estate;
> Behold rather the sweetness of his sorrow –
> may increase a thousand fold!
> Jalaleddinm Rumi (Molavi)

CHAPTER TWENTY-EIGHT ENDNOTES

1.	Mir Ghotbeddin Mohammad Angha, *From Fetus to Paradise*, Marvi Offset Publication, Teheran, 1965 p. 3.

2.	Salaheddin Ali Nader Angha, *Mystery of Humanity*. United Press of America, 1986, introduction, p. 3.

CHAPTER TWENTY-NINE

THE FLIGHT BACK HOME

I have created you free.

Holy Koran

Totally dependent upon the law and forces of nature, man does not possess free will, and it is an error to think so. One might think that having an opinion and a right to deny or accept the truth means free will, but the Truth and the Law govern man's very existence.

Let us be honest and ask ourselves: "How much power does one have over one's own body and mind?" Now let's extend the question to one's household and family members, then to one's city, country, and then entire existence! Can we decide not to breathe or not to eat or drink or sleep? Given all these limitations, what kind of free will are we talking about?

On the contrary, the freedom we think we are exercising is actually captivity. If one looks closely, one sees everything is preplanned for us. Let's start with our name and religion, which are decided on and chosen for us at birth (or even before birth). Our roles and goals are dictated by society, even including what we should think and say.

As we grow up, we become disconnected from the true spring of life, which gives birth to love and creativity. We become trapped and must conform to the laws of society what we should say, even what we should wear is decided for us, first by one's parents, then teachers and then society and media. We become a mere puppet, a mechanical figure led by the wheels of the economic structure and social standards. Each person becomes a carbon copy of the next.

"Children are very creative," says Roger Van Oech, author of *Whack on the Side of the Head*. "Watch a baby and what you will see is amazing. As we get older, most of us lose a good deal of that innate creativity." "Research underlines this," adds Robert McGarvey, who writes about methods of achieving success. "In one test of creativity 84 percent of five-year-olds rank high. By second grade, however, just 10 percent are creative". As for the reasons behind this dramatic drop, Von Oech says there are many a school system that insists there is just one right answer, when often there are many. If you believe there is only one right answer, you'll stop looking as soon as you come up with your first answer.

"Other factors come into play as well," says Eugene Raudsepp, president of Princeton Creative Research in New Jersey, pointing to another cause of loss of creativity. "Conformity kills creativity, and the pressures to 'not to rock the boat' are frequently strong in school, the family, the workplace. We don't want to be different, but that is what creativity is."[1]

In the *Principles of Faghr and Sufism*, Hazrat Shah Maghsoud says:

> The contamination of our thoughts starts from birth as a result of attempting to conform to and adapt ourselves to our environment. The child, in order to adapt himself to his environment, becomes contemplative, enchanted, and pensive and falls out of his true inner being. The acquisition that the child gains during this hurricane of events results in the loss of all chances to return to his true source of innate knowledge and the ability of pure reflection. This is because the child accepts and obeys the imposed world as the inherent agent of an unchangeable destiny. Thus, his life remains static and meaningless as he blindly starts building his folklore, religious beliefs, his goals and finally, his death. He becomes enchanted with the appearance of things, and blindly obeys the commands of the senses and emotions and replaces actions and reactions for the truth and reality. Because he is ignorant of the knowledge within himself, he has become short-sighted and erroneous. He wrongly uses Truth as a means of satisfying his sensual desires and is like a glutton who finally passes away at his own table.[2]

Many talk about *freedom*. The freedom to be able to do whatever their senses command is sheer *slavery*! Today, what is meant by freedom seems to be the liberty of *becoming like everyone else*. This is not called freedom. Being yourself and being allowed to grow according to the best of your potential and qualities is freedom. Each individual has so much to find within himself and so much to give to society as a result.

"Each human being is like a mine...gold, silver or jewel,"[3] says the prophet of Islam. To excavate one's inner wealth is what the prophets have to say to us. To know and discover the source of life in you and to grow accordingly is freedom. The Sufi Master Hazrat Shah Maghsoud was asked, "What should I do?" He replied, "Be who you are is all you should do!"

"The development of science and of the creative activities of the spirit in general requires still another kind of freedom which may be characterized as inward freedom," says Einstein. "It is this freedom of the spirit which consists in the independence of thought from the restrictions of authoritarian and social prejudices as well as from unphilosophical routinizing and habit in general. This inward freedom is an infrequent gift of nature and a worthy objective for the individual."[4]

For man it is humiliating to have to compete with machinery and to spend a whole lifetime reaching toward a goal that is purely economic and material. It is true that man's physical needs should be considered, but to devote a lifetime to satisfying desires and physical needs, never wondering who he is underneath the skin, never asking who it is that looks through his eyes, who loves, who feels, who cries. He is always striving, never satisfied, never proud, his hungry soul longing for spiritual nourishment.

To separate man from his divine origin is to chain him and to take away his freedom and his birthright, just as trapping and caging a bird deprives it of its birthright and the freedom to fly. Do we not deserve also to taste liberty? Do we not deserve to regain and enjoy the celestial beauty and the freedom we enjoyed before falling into the prison of our senses? Rumi says,

> Within the egg of the body you are a marvelous bird,
> Since you are inside the egg,
> You cannot fly.

> If the body's shell should break,
> You will flap your wings and win the spirit.

> Oh man! This body keeps you in torment
> The bird of your spirit is imprisoned with a bird
> of another kind.
>
> The spirit is a falcon, but bodily dispositions are crows,
> The falcon has received many wounds from
> crows and owls.
>
> When will the bird of my spirit fly from the cage,
> toward the garden?
>
> The only thing that will keep a caged bird
> from trying to fly is ignorance.[5]

Freedom, in the School of Islamic Sufism, MTO, is liberation from all bondage: the flight back home. "I have created you free" *(Enna khalaghnakom horra)*, God says in the Koran.

Freedom is to be freed of desires and attachments. These are the chains that hold us down and make our flight home impossible. Hazrat Shah Maghsoud explains,

> Desires are endless, and people are not satisfied with what they have, no matter what they have. Desires are like sandy deserts; their invisible extremes are extended to deep oceans. No matter how much water is poured they still remain dry and thirsty. Whose thoughts can saturate and irrigate these endless sands? Only a fool's. A man who is infatuated and deceived by his dreams and wishes will not enjoy the present moment and always worries about a vague future.
>
> The strongest bond that makes man interested in this world and its attachments is ignorance. Knowledge and ignorance are two different states that extend toward different extremes. A man who chooses knowledge will not get lost in sensual joys and attachments, but the other will find nothing but wandering. A learned man, who has found himself, will not get lost in joy or sadness. He is free, more or less, from good and bad, the present and future.[6]

"Are you the victor, the self-conqueror, the ruler of your senses, the Lord of your virtues?" asks Nietzsche. "Or do animal and necessity speak from your desire? Or isolation? Or disharmony in yourself."[7]

If man is bound to his lowest nature, he will never find satisfaction. The satisfaction of primary needs such as food, sex, and security is not the ideal for man, only for animals. There is a difference, although many claim otherwise, between the needs of man and animals. To live like an animal is to deprive man of his birthright and his true identity. Man has other needs and much inner potential has to be discovered in order to live a fulfilled and enriching life. For man is greater than animal. He may know the spirit that gave birth to him; animals may not. Animals are in fact living up to their fullest potential, and their natural requirements and instincts.

Man needs to grow, to be creative, to feel good about the person he is, and to set his own standards. Why should he have to obey the standards society imposes on him? Instead of trying to adapt constantly to the standards that society places upon him, man should tend to his deeper needs. Man needs to know himself. "Any thought that is not meant for inner peace and tranquility is useless, and worthless is knowledge that enhances not the personality."[8]

A healthy lifestyle, personal introspection, contemplation, and meditation are necessary and will enrich the quality of life. These will help us know ourselves and truly understand our most human needs. Only through such self-knowledge can we achieve the growth, harmony, and tranquility whose attainment are the purpose of life. Only through such self-knowledge can we become strong, balanced, able to withstand the increasing pressures of life. When man re-establishes his connection with the source of knowledge within himself, he then becomes the architect of his environment and this involves a very broad spectrum, beginning within and extending to the society and the environment around him. But if his existence, his thoughts and actions depend and are based on environmental influences, an unstable source outside of him, he will shape his life according to those standards. As a consequence, he will be like a man who has built his house on sand that has no firm basis; his investment, his fortune is lost, evidence of which will surface in his environment within and without.

Through meditation this connection takes place. We can say all we want, but only the meditator will experience it. Until meditation is practiced, it remains a myth or a word, the meaning of which is not clear and might arouse different feelings, ideas, and presumptions in different people. "This is the image many people have of meditation: You sit in a full lotus posture and pretend you're a Buddha," laments Jon Kabat-Zinn, Ph.D., director of the University of Massachusetts Medical Center's relaxation program.[9]

Feelings, ideas, and presumptions are so changeable that we cannot really depend on them. We must experience the truth. Even the best theoretical knowledge cannot serve as a basis for judgment, for that which is described remains to be discovered; until then it will be but a pale symbol of the real thing. Theoretical knowledge alone is as a rose without the scent.

Islam is the call for freedom, not for men or women, black or white, but for mankind, for souls imprisoned in the cage of attachments. It is the final stage of self-knowledge; it is the surrender to the ultimate truth, God, and its discovery within oneself. It is this submission to God that makes one a Muslim, not certain outward actions reflecting traditions, politics, or social behaviors. The first Muslim according to the Koran is the prophet Abraham. His total surrender to God marks the stage of Islam. He is the one who built the Ka'ba, the house of God in Mecca, that the pilgrims go to visit. This house was an outer sign of the one he had first built for God within his heart. The return to that home within to join the long lost Father, as did Abraham under the guidance of the wise architect, the Messenger within, is our goal. The return of the soul to its eternal abode where it can live on after the destruction of the mortal body is the goal.

Molavi, the Sufi poet, says:

The great scholars of the age split hairs in all the sciences. They have gained total knowledge and complete mastery of things that have nothing to do with them. But that which is important and closer to him than anything else, namely his own self, this your great scholar does not know.

Wretched humanity! Not knowing his own self, man has come from a high estate and fallen into lowliness! He has sold himself cheaply; he was satin, yet he has sewn himself onto a tattered cloak. If you could only see your own beauty – for you are greater than the sun! Why are you withered and shriveled in this prison of dust? Why not become fresh from the gentleness of the heart's spring? Why not laugh like a rose? Why not spread perfume?[10]

CHAPTER TWENTY-NINE ENDNOTES

1.   Robert McGarvey , "Creative Thinking," *US Air Magazine*, June 1990, p. 34.

2.   Shah Maghsoud Sadegh Angha, *The Principles of Faghr and Sufism*, MTO Publication, Verdugo City, Ca., 1987, p. 50.

3.   Hazrat Mohammad, *Nahjol – Fessaheh*.

4.   Albert Einstein , *Out of My Later Years*, 1990, New York, p. 13.

5.   William C. Chittick, *The Sufi Path of Love*, State University of New York Press, Albany, 1983, p. 25.

6.   Shah Maghsoud Sadegh Angha, *The Manifestation of Thought*, ETRI Publication, San Rafael, Ca. 1980.

7.   Frederick Nietzsche, *Thus Spoke Zarathustra*, Penguin Books Ltd., NY, 1982, p. 95.

8.   Shah Maghsoud Sadegh Angha, *Psalm of Gods*, from the collection *The Mystery of Humanity*, University Press of America, Inc., Lanham, MD, 1986, p. 51.

9.   *Washington Post*, "Meditation Goes Mainstream," October 1987.

10.   Chittick, p. 149.

BIBLIOGRAPHY

Ali, Hazrat, Seyed Jafery, trans., *Najul Balagha*, P.O. Box 1115, Elmhurst, New York, 1978, sermon; 130.

Angha, Mohammad Mir Ghotbeddin, *From Fetus to Paradise*, Moravi Offset Publication, Tehran, Iran, 1965.

Angha, Salaheddin Ali Nader, *The Wealth of Solouk and The Secret Word*, M.T.O. Shah Maghsoudi Publications, San Rafael, CA, 1984.

Angha, Salaheddin Ali Nader, *Massnavi Ravayeh*, University Press of America, Inc., 1990.

Angha, Salaheddin Ali Nader, *The Mystery of Humanity*. UPA 1986, p. 3 of Introduction.

Angha, Salaheddin Ali Nader, *Peace*, M.T.O. Publication, Box 209, Verdugo City, CA., 91046, 1987.

Angha, Shah Maghsoud Sadegh, *Dawn (Sahar)*, University Press of America, Inc., 4720, Lanham, MD, 20706, 1989.

Angha, Shah Maghsoud Sadegh, *The Epic of Existence*, Persian edition, Behjat Publication, 1974.

Angha, Shah Maghsoud Sadegh, *Ghazaliat*, M.T.O. Publication, Tehran, Iran, 1985.

Angha, Shah Maghsoud Sadegh, *The Hidden Angles of Life*, Multidisciplinary Publications, Pomona, CA.

Angha, Shah Maghsoud Sadegh, *Al Rasael*, University Press of America, Inc., 1978.

Angha, Shah Maghsoud Sadegh, *The Manifestation of Thought*, ETRI Publications, San Rafael, CA, 1980.

Angha, Shah Maghsoud Sadegh, *The Manifestation of Thought*, UPA Publication, 1988.

Angha, Shah Maghsoud Sadegh, *The Message from the Soul*, University Press of America, Inc., 1986.

Angha, Shah Maghsoud Sadegh, *Nirvan*, University Press of America, Inc., 1986.

Angha, Shah Maghsoud Sadegh, *The Principles of Faghr and Sufism*, Verdugo City, CA., M.T.O. Publication, 1987.

Angha, Shah Maghsoud Sadegh, *Psalm of Gods*, UPA Publication, 1986.

Angha, Shah Maghsoud Sadegh, *The States of Enlightenment*, University Press of America, Inc., Lanham, MD, 1986.

Bloomfield, Harold H., et al., *TM Discovering Inner Energy and Overcoming Stress*, Delacorte Press, New York, 1975.

Bouddhin, Rev. Lawrence, et al., *Meditation in Christianity*, Himalayan Publishers, Honesdale, Pennsylvania, 1983.

Buddha, *Dhammapada*, trans. Irving Babbit, NDP, NY.

Chatterji, J. C., *The Wisdom of the Vedas*, The Theosophical Publishing House, Wheaton, Illinois, 1949.

Chittick, William C., *The Sufi Path of Love*, State University of New York Press, Albany, New York, 1983.

Einstein, Albert, *Out of My Later Years*, Bonanza Books, New York, 1990.

Grisel, Ronald, *Sufism*. Ross Books Publication, 1983, CA, 94704.

Guthrie, W. K. C., *The Greek Philosophers*, Harper Torch Books, London, 1950.

Hawking, W. Stephen, *A Brief History of Time*, A Bantam Book, New York, 1988.

Jung, C. Carl, *Thoughts Reflections, Dreams*.

Lederman, Leon M. and D. N. Schramm, *From Quarks to Cosmos*, Scientific America, Library, 1989.

Mohammad, Hazrat, *Nahjol-Fessaheh*, Persian edition.

Mohammad, Hazrat, *Holy Hadith*, M.T.O. Publication, San Rafael, 1985.

Nietzsche, Frederick, *Thus Spoke Zarathustra*, Penguin Books Ltd., NY, 1982.

Nizami, Ganjavi, *Complete Poetical Works*, Zarren Publication, Persian edition, Tehran, Iran.

O'Becker, Robert, M.D. and Gary Seldon, *The Body Electric*, Quill, New York, NY, 1985.

Parrender, Geoffrey, ed., *World Religions, from Ancient History to the Present*, Fact on File Publications, New York, NY, 1983.

Pelletier, Kenneth R., *Mind as Healer, Mind as Slayer*, Dell Publishing Company Inc., New York, NY, 1977.

Rumi, Jalaleddinm, *Massnavi Manavi*, Persian edition, Sepehr Pub., 1925, page 716.

Russell, Bertrand, *A History of Western Philosophy*, Simon & Schuster Pub., 1945, Rockefeller Center, New York, NY.

Swami Rama, Ajaya, *Yoga and Psychotherapy*, Himalayan International Institute, Honesdale, PA, 1981.

Schwartz, Jack, *Human Energy Systems*, E. P. Dutton, New York, NY, 1980.

Schwartz, Jackie, *Letting go of Stress*, Pinnacle Books, Inc., New York, NY 10018, 1982.

Shaigan, Dariush, *Religious & Philosophical School of India*, Tehran, Iran, 1977.

Shirazi Hafiz, Shamseddin, *Fifty Poems of Hafiz*, Arthur J. Arberry, transl., Cambridge University Press, 1947.

Shirazi Hafiz, Shamseddin, *Odes*, Mazda Publication, Lexington, KY, USA, 1984.

Suzuki, D. T., *Essays on Zen Buddhism*, Grove Press, Inc., New York, 1985.

Tournier, Paul, Edwin Hudson, trans., *The Healing of Persons*, Harper & Row Publishers, Inc., New York, NY.

Uthman, Ali Bin, *Kahf-Al-Mahjub*, Islamic Book Foundation, Lahore, 1976.

Watts, Alan, *The Way of Zen*, Random House, New York, NY, 1957.

Wood, Earnest, *Concentration, An Approach to Meditation*, Theosophical Publishing House, Wheaton, Illinois, 1949.

The Encyclopedia Britannica, Grolier Inc., New York, 1974.

Encyclopedia International. Groliker Inc., New York 1974.

Encyclopedia of Philosophy, Macmillan Publishing.

Random House Dictionary of the English Language.

Encyclopedia of Religion and Ethics, edited by James Hastings, Charles Scribner's Sons Publication.

Word Book Dictionary.

Hinnels, John R., ed., *The Dictionary of Religions* (from Abraham to Zoroaster), Penguin Books Ltd., Middlesex, England, 1984.

236

Ali, Abdullah Yusufi, transl., *The Holy Koran*, Amana Corp., Maryland, USA, 1983.

The New Oxford Annotated Bible (revised edition), Oxford University Press, 1962.

Oxford Universal Dictionary on Historical Principles, Oxford University Press, Amen House, London, England, 1955.

The Oxford English Dictionary, Oxford Press, Amen House, London, England, 1961.

US Air Magazine, June 1990.

US Air Magazine, August 1990.

Discover Magazine, April 1986, page 22.

Discover Magazine, February 1987, page 51.

Washington Post, February 17, 1987, page 8.

Washington Post, October 1987.

For more information about the worldwide classes,
centers and locations of

MTO Shah Maghsoudi, School of Islamic Sufism,
please write to:

MTO Shah Maghsoudi

Department of Meditation and Healing
P.O. Box 26866
San Diego, California 92196